I0102291

THE CHRISTIAN STATE

A

Christian State
For the Middle East

By

Gene Schwimmer

Copyright © 2008 Eugene Allan Schwimmer

All rights reserved, including the right to reproduce this book or portions thereof in any form whatsoever.

Contact Gene Schwimmer at gene@thechristianstate.com.

TABLE OF CONTENTS

The plight of Christian minorities in the Middle East is one of the 20th century tragedies to which we pay least attention. — Stephen Crittenden[1]

For too long the plight of Christian Arabs has been put on the back-burner or ignored altogether." — Rev. Malcolm Hedding[2]

The Christian community has suffered because we are a minority. — Father Pierbattista Pizzabella[3]

Western countries have been supportive of the self-determination campaigns of Muslims, especially Christians. – Rev. Keith Roderick

[A]s far as the 'peace process' is concerned, Christians are notable by their absence! — Walid Phares[4]

---

[1] Stephen Crittenden, "Christian Minorities in the Islamic Middle East: Rosie Malek-Yonan on the Assyrians," *The Religion Report*, interview, May 30, 2007, on ABC Radio National (Australia). Available online at http://www.abc.net.au/rn/religionreport/stories/2007/1937124.htm.
[2] Etgar Levkovits, "Expert: Christian groups in PA to disappear," *Jerusalem Post*, December 4, 2007.
[3] Harry de Quetteville, "'Islamic Mafia' accused of persecuting Holy Land Christians," *Daily Telegraph* (London), September 9, 2005.
[4] Walid Phares, "Middle East Christians: The Captive Nations," in Malka Hillel Shulewitz, ed., *The Forgotten Millions: The Modern Jewish Exodus from Arab Lands* (London: Continuum, 1999), p. 25.

INTRODUCTION

I wrote this book to argue that the time has come to establish a Christian state in Middle East, to dwell peacefully beside Israel and to enable Christians, after being denied for thousands of years, to take their place as equals to the other monotheistic faiths in the Holy Land.

I also wrote it because I am alarmed at the widespread persecution of Christians throughout the world and world's willful (in my opinion) refusal even to acknowledge, let alone deal with, it. With each passing year, the Christians' plight grows worse and with each passing year, that plight remains "one of the tragedies to which we pay the least attention."

Could it be that we in the West, are less compassionate than we like to think we are? I would like to claim not, but the evidence, at least as far as the world's persecuted Christians is concerned, argues persuasively to the contrary.

Perhaps understandably, it can be hard to think of members of a faith with 2.6 billion adherents as a "persecuted minority," but in fact, in many countries — Muslim countries (and one non-Muslim country, India)--that is exactly what they are. In many countries where Christians are a minority, Christians suffer terribly from harassment, discrimination, persecution, violence and even death.

And of all the world's persecuted Christians, few suffer as much, and none suffers more, than Christian Palestinians, a powerless minority, forced against its will, to endure the consequences of the Muslim Palestinians' holy war against the Jews.

This book is my lonely attempt to get the international community to see what it goes out of its way *not* to see: the persecuted Christians of Judea and Samaria (deliberately misnamed, for political reasons, as we shall see presently, the "West Bank" and "occupied territories") and the Gaza strip. Why does the international community ignore them? That, too, is the subject of this book.

In this book, I make the obvious comparison, likening the plight of today's Christian Palestinians, to that of their predecessors, the Jewish Palestinians of pre-1948 Israel. Of course, few historical comparisons are 100%. Zionist-era Jewish Palestinians did not endure nearly the suffering then that Christian Palestinians endure today, as evidenced by the facts that the Jewish Palestinian population increased throughout the Zionist era, while the Christian Palestinian population, under the Muslim Palestinian Authority, has been declining rapidly, to the point where Bethlehem's later mayor, Elias Freij could predict a time when Bethlehem would be "a town with churches but no Christians." (Oh, and by the way, for those of you who may be wondering: Since 1948, the Christian population of Israel, under majority-Jewish rule, has tripled.)

Why Christian Palestinians have it so much worse today than Jewish Palestinians—today's Israelis—matters. First, in the years preceding Israel's re-declaration of independence, the British Mandate was administered by, obviously, the British, who, though clearly prejudiced in favor of the Muslim Palestinians, did, for the most part, maintain order. Christian Palestinians, on the other hand, live under direct Muslim Palestinian (mis)rule. Second, the Jewish Palestinians had their own militia, the Palmah, progenitor of the Israel Defense Forces, to defend them when the British would not; Christian Palestinians have no such militias.

And of course, Jewish Palestinians fare far better than Muslim Palestinians 60 years after they distinguished themselves from the Muslims as a *separate* people, Israelis, with a full-fledged army, navy and air force to defend them, behind distinct borders, *in an independent state*. Consequently, 4.5 million Middle Eastern Jews are strong and secure, while 14 million Christians—not just in Judea, Samaria and Gaza, but dispersed throughout the Middle East, are weak and anything but secure.

Which brings us to my main purpose for writing this book: my strong belief that the *only* thing that will secure the safety of Middle Eastern Christians, especially those of Judea, Samaria and Gaza; the *only* thing that will allow them to live in peace, prosperity and security; the *only* thing that will not only arrest the Christian population's decline, but allow it to flourish; the *only* thing that will allow Christianity to take its rightful, *equal* place alongside Judaism and Islam in the Middle East; and finally, the only thing that will provide a guarantee sanctuary for the world's persecuted Christians, wherever situated; is an *independent Middle Eastern Christian state.*

*   *   *

I invite all to write to me at gene@thechristianstate.com and to visit my Web site, updated when relevant events warrant, www.thechristianstate.com.

WHAT IS A "CHRISTIAN STATE"?

Now you may ask: When I say "Christian state," what am I talking about? Are there not, already, many Christian states? Is The United States not a Christian state? Is not Europe comprised entirely of Christian states?

The answer, emphatically, is *no*. There is a profound difference between a Christian *majority* state, and a *Christian* state. A Christian state is a Christian state in precisely the same way that Israel is a Jewish state. As in Israel, all faiths are equally respected, but a Christian state would display the cross on her flag as proudly as Israel displays the Star of David on hers.

Most important for our purpose—providing a sanctuary for the word's persecuted Christians—a Christian state would have the equivalent of Israel's Law of Return, whereby, as is the case with Jews emigrating to Israel, any Christian, with only the rarest exceptions, would be granted automatic admittance and citizenship.

A LITTLE HOUSEKEEPING

Before I can proceed with my argument, I must, as a Jew, attend to a couple of matters of terminology deliberately concocted by Israel's and my people's enemies and detractors to deny our historic attachment and historic right to "Eretz Israel" — and by that, I mean *all* of Israel, both the land comprising the modern state and the ancient kingdom that preceded it and of which we forcibly deprived for 2,000 years.

First, as I did at the end of the preceding chapter, unless I am repeating a direct quote or the context clearly requires it, I shall dispense with the historically meaningless, politically-motivated term, "West Bank" and refer to the area by it's historically correct names: Judea (the southern portion) and Samaria (the northern portion):

> Judea and Samaria, located west of the Jordan River, with Jerusalem approximately in the center, are historical parts of the Land of Israel. They are currently called the "West Bank", *a name created by Jordan after the War of Independence in 1948* when Arab armies overran Judea and Samaria. Despite the fact that virtually the entire world rejected Jordan's annexation, and even after Israel drove the occupiers back across the river in the 1967 Six Day War, the phrase "West Bank" has stuck, and is used to the near total exclusion of any other.

The mountains of Judea are first named in the Book of Joshua, in the account of the conquering of Canaan by the Israelites during the creation of the Land of Israel. From that time to the present, more than 3,000 years, the name Judea has been consistently used to describe the territory from Jerusalem south along the Judean mountain ridge line, extending east from the mountains down to the Dead Sea.

The hill country north and west of Jerusalem has been known as Samaria since the days of King Jeroboam, first king of the breakaway ten northern tribes of Israel after the death of King Solomon.

Judea and Samaria have been known by these names for unbroken centuries, and were registered as such on official documents and maps, by international institutions and in authoritative reference books right up to about 1950. *When the correct names became a problem for Palestinian Arabs trying to make their newly-minted claim on the land, it somehow became "politically correct" to use "West Bank" or "occupied territories" instead of the historically accurate names Judea and Samaria.*[1]

But we need not go back that far. The following examples illustrate how recently, in modern times, people referred to Judea and Samaria by their proper, historically accurate names:

- A map published by the US State Department designating the Middle East's "Military Situation" on July 18, 1948 calls the

---

[1] "What do the names Judea and Samaria refer to?" *Palestinian Facts,* http://www.palestinefacts.org/pf_early_palestine_judea_samaria.php. (emphasis added)

"Arab held" area north of Jerusalem "Samaria."

- In A Survey of Palestine prepared by the Anglo-American Committee of Inquiry in December 1945 and January 1946 the authors used the titles "Judea" and "Samaria" as a matter of course when referring to what later became the "West Bank."

- In United Nations General Assembly Resolution 181 adopted November 29, 1947, the world body calls Judea and Samaria by those historical names.

- Every edition of the Encyclopedia Britannica, [at least up to the 1994] writes extensively concerning the areas politically called the West Bank, and calls them by their historically accurate names: Samaria and Judea. The fact that the "West Bank" is not mentioned once in the 1954 edition of the Encyclopedia Britannica indicates just how recently this title entered popular usage.[2]

The need for my second "housekeeping task" is best illustrated by the following letter, sent to the *New York Times* in 1975:

Dear Sir:

Your newspaper frequently uses the term "Palestinian" to describe a section of the Middle East population which is Arab, to differentiate it from Israeli Jews. As the holder of a *Palestinian Identity Card and a Certificate of Discharge from a Palestinian Unit of the British army*, I find this practice annoying and certainly untrue.

---

[2] Ibid.

We Palestinian Jews wore the uniform of the British Army, and on our shoulder epaulettes the single word, "Palestine" in English. We tried to get permission to wear Hebrew insignia, fly the Jewish flag and be recognized as Palestinian Jews, but no, Palestinian meant Jew *and* Arab and who cared if there were fewer than 3,000 Arabs as compared to 36,000 Jews in khaki? In British army nomenclature, the equivalent of a GI is BOR, meaning British Other Rank. We were formally known as POR, Palestinian Other Ranks.

So we fought the war as Palestinians, set up the Jewish Brigade as Palestinians, and *I'll be damned if I agree that only Arafat[3] and his assassins are Palestinians.*

As a Palestinian, I was arrested by the British on suspicion of smuggling immigrants into the country. As a Palestinian, I had the honor of commanding the 329th Palestinian Company of the Royal Electrical and Mechanical Engineers (all Jews). There were no equivalent Arab units. Once a British general said to me, "Migawd, I have so many things to dislike you for, for being a Jew, American born, *a Palestinian* — and you don't even know how to handle a knife and fork!

So cut it out, please. Call them what you will, but not Palestinians.

Yours truly,

Joe Criden[4]

---

[3] Who, incidentally, was Egyptian. Arafat was born in Cairo.
[4] Joe Criden, Letter to the *New York Times* (unpublished), Arthur Kahn and Thomas Murray, The Palestinians: A Political Masquerade, published by Americans for a Safe Israel. Available online at http://www.afsi.org/MEDIA/newsLinks/shockers/m100.htm.

The *Times*, to its discredit, declined to publish Criden's letter, but his point was, and is, a good one, a point further reinforced a mere two years after Joe Criden wrote his letter, by no less than Zuheir Mohsein, at that time, a Member of the Supreme Council of the Palestinian Liberation Organization, who freely admitted in 1977:

> There are no differences between Jordanians, Palestinians, Syrians and Lebanese. We are all part of one nation. *It is only for political reasons* that we carefully underline our Palestinian identity, because it is in the interests of the Arabs to encourage a separate Palestinian identity in contrast to Zionism. Yes, the existence of a separate Palestinian identity is there *only for tactical reasons.*[5]

Conversely, as Rachel Neuwirth explains:

> The Israelis are not colonists or alien "settlers" in the Land of Israel with no past connection or relationship to the country; on the contrary, we Jews have lived in Israel for at least 3,200 years if not longer. This is far longer than most peoples have lived in their present national homelands. Our two glorious temples, wonders of the ancient world, were there for a thousand years. King David's kingdom endured for more than four hundred years; later, there was an independent Jewish state of the Maccabees. Jews had lived in the Land of Israel in large numbers for at least 1,800 years before the Arabs conquered it in 635 C.E. Moreover, while hundreds of thousands of Jews were expelled from their land or put to death in it by foreign conquerors, there have been at least some Jews living there almost continuously for 3,200 years.

[5] *Trouw* (Dutch newspaper), March 31, 1977. (emphases mine)

> There has never been a distinctive "Palestinian" Arab people or an Arab "Palestine" state or nation; while it is true that some Arabs have lived in the Land of Israel for many centuries, they have never been ethnically or culturally distinct or different from the Arabs who live in other lands, including the original Arab homeland, the Arabian Peninsula. *The Jews, however, are people who originated in the Land of Israel and never had any other national homeland.*[6]

Having no interest in helping Fatah and Hamas replace my ancient homeland with a bogus "Palestinian state," the term, "Palestinian," when not appearing in a direct quote or required by context, includes Muslims, Christians *and Jews.* That Jewish Palestinians now proudly call themselves "Israelis" does not change the fact that they are every bit as "Palestinian" as self-named Muslim and Christian "Palestinians," with an equal *and earlier* claim to the land Similarly, I will eschew phrasing such as "Palestinians and Israelis," in favor of the more accurate "Muslim Palestinians, Christian Palestinians and Israelis," or "Muslim Palestinians, Christian Palestinians and Jewish Palestinians."

Finally, a note about the term, "Christian state." Though that is the entity I advocate, I am not a Christian and I realize that some Christian denominations may have a theological objection to creating a full-fledged state. Evangelicals, for example, at least where parts of what was once Israel is concerned, might believe that Jews must be sovereign over the entirety of our ancient homeland to herald the return of their Messiah. Catholics might feel that the Christian Savior calls them out of earthly nations to form a new nation, of heaven.

---

[6] Rachel Neuwirth, "But what Can I Do About the Crisis Facing Israel and the Jewish People?" *American Thinker*, March 9, 2008. (emphasis added)

Christians who object to a Christian state on theological grounds should take my use of the term "Christian state" as one of convenience. I am certain, if the will is there, that there are "theologically legal" ways to create a *de facto*, but not *de jure* Christian state. For example, in the case of one suggested site, Judea, Christians could lease the area from Israel for, say, a thousand years or until the Second Coming, whichever occurs first, for one, for the price of one Israeli shekel. Or the area(s) chosen for the Christian state could be deemed an "Israeli protectorate" or "autonomous Christian enclave" and its defense forces could be deemed a branch of the Israel Defense Forces, whose soldiers wear Israeli uniforms.

The goal is freedom, security and self-determination for the Middle East's Christians, and sanctuary for persecuted Christians everywhere; the legal structure of entity that provides it is immaterial. But in this book, for now, I will use the term, "Christian state."

*   *   *

And now, with all of my little housekeeping tasks out of the way, I can begin my argument demonstrating the need for a Christian state by showing what life is like, today, *without a Christian state*, for all too many Christians.

PERSECUTION OF BORN CHRISTIANS[1]

It is not rare even today that we receive news from various parts of the world of missionaries, priests, bishops, monks, nuns and lay people persecuted, imprisoned, tortured, deprived of their liberty or prevented from exercising it because they are disciples of Christ and apostles of the Gospel — Pope Benedict XVI[2]

Judea, Samaria and Gaza

In 1990, when Yasser Arafat was still sipping coffee in Tunisia and Israel controlled all of Judea, Samaria and Gaza, Bethlehem was 60 percent Christian. By 2006, the Christians' numbers had been whittled down to a mere 12 percent of a total population of 60,000.[3] It did not happen by accident. As part of a deliberate campaign to reduce Christian representation in the city of their Savior's birth, Arafat redrew Bethlehem's boundaries to incorporate three refugee camps, comprising 30,000 Muslims, plus additional thousands from a nearby Bedouin tribe and from Hebron, transforming the Christian majority into a minority, virtually overnight. Next came large construction projects, in the very heart of the town, to house this massive influx of Muslims.[4] When nine Christian city council members resigned rather than approve the construction, Arafat replaced them with

---

[1] "Born Christians" means Christians born into the faith, as distinguished from Christians who convert from another faith and whom I shall treat in a separate section.
[2] Robin Pomeroy, "Pope hails persecuted Christians as modern martyrs," *Reuters*, December 26, 2007.
[3] Elizabeth Day, "O, Muslim Town of Bethlehem…," *Daily Mail* (London), December 16, 2006)
[4] And yet, these same Muslim Palestinians complain about Israeli "settlements." How does one say "chutzpah" in Arabic?

Muslims, changing the council's composition from majority-Christian to 50:50, and, for good measure, installed a Muslim as Governor of the Bethlehem District.[5]

Hamas

By 2005, a systematic, *de facto* collusion was underway between the Palestinian Authority (PA) and an "Islamic fundamentalist mafia" to intimidate West Bank and Gazan Christians.[6] You probably know that "Islamic fundamentalist mafia" by its more familiar name: Hamas.

Hamas ran on a platform of confronting the rampant corruption brought on by Arafat's governing party, Fatah. But once in power, Hamas wasted no time revealing its real goals: the elimination of Israel and, most dire for the area's Christians, the transformation of Gaza into an Iranian-style Islamic theocracy, with Iranian-style harassment of non-Muslims.

Extortion and Harassment of Christian Palestinians

In today's "Hamastan," Christian businesses — the ones that Muslim boycotts have not yet forced out of business — are routinely subject to extortion. "I know many businessmen who have been extorted," says one Christian. "There wasn't a Christian businessman exempt."[7] One Christian café owner who refused to pay protection money — the infamous *jizyah*, the historic poll tax levied on non-Muslims in Muslim societies — was branded a "collaborator," shot in the eye and forced to emigrate.[8] In another instance, a Christian Armenian gold dealer had traveled to Gaza to sell some gold jewelry. Despite having all the required licenses, the Palestinian Authority police arrested him, took him to an interrogation room, and beat

[5] David Raab, "The Beleaguered Christians of the Palestinian-Controlled Ares, *Jerusalem Center for Public Affairs*, January 1-15, 2003, http://www.jcpa.org/jl/vp490 .htm.
[6] Dore Gold, *The Fight for Jerusalem* (Washington, D.C.: Regnery Publishing, Inc., 2007), 211, citing Harry de Quetteville.
[7] Justus Reid Weiner, 11-12.
[8] Ibid., 12.

him for six to seven hours before offering him the "opportunity" to give up half his gold. When he refused, the policemen beat him for two hours more. Ultimately, the police got their half share—and the dealer's watch, rings and $6,000 in cash. During the ordeal, the police left no doubt that everything that was done to the dealer was done because he was not a Muslim: a Muslim would have been protected by his connections with the Muslim authorities.[9]

Islamic Fundamentalism on the Rise

"Creeping Islamic fundamentalism"[10] is making life increasingly miserable for Judea's Christian Palestinians. For example, near Bethlehem sits a Greek Orthodox shrine that, in more peaceful times, when Israel controlled the area, enjoyed visits from members of all three of the monotheistic faiths. Today, with the Israelis gone and Fatah in charge, no one visits, the structure has fallen into neglect and the priest has had to close the church out of fear that Muslims would turn it into a mosque.[11]

Here is how Lina Atallah, a Christian receptionist at the Silesian Convent and Church, describes living among Muslims in increasingly fundamentalist Muslim "Palestine": "They spit at us, try to force us to wear headscarves, and in the [Islamic] fasting month of Ramadan . . . the Palestinian police even arrest us for smoking or eating on the streets. . . . The Muslims want . . . us to live like them."[12]

Bethlehem, the Christian Savior's birthplace, becomes less Christian with each passing day. A Greek Orthodox church still sits in Manger Square, as does a Roman Catholic one. But on the other side of the square is a mosque. The shutters on the Christian souvenir shops are painted green, the

9 Ibid., 12.
10 Elizabeth Day.
11 Sandro Magister, *The Custody Must Be Doubled in the Holy Land,* September 7, 2005, *www.chiesa,* *http://www.chiesa.espresso.repubblica.it/ dettaglio.jsp?id=38551 &eng=y.*
12 Justus Reid Weiner, 10.

traditional color of Islam. Visitors to Bethlehem at Christmastime can see a Christmas tree in the Al-Jacir Palace Hotel lobby—and in each room, a card showing the direction of Mecca.

Muslim Violation of Churches

There are numerous instances of Muslims vandalizing churches and stealing crucifixes. A statue of the Virgin Mary was destroyed. Tombs have been desecrated.[13] Gaza's only public Christian library has been torched. Twice.[14]

Yasser Arafat turned a Greek Orthodox monastery near the Church of the Nativity into a domicile for his personal use when visiting Bethlehem.[15] His Palestine Liberation Organization forcibly evicted monks and nuns from another monastery in Hebron.[16]

The al-Hanake Mosque sits adjacent to one of Christendom's holiest shrines, the Church of the Holy Sepulcher, revered by the faithful as the tomb where Jesus' physical body was entombed before Jesus' ascension to heaven. In 1997, workers for the mosque broke into the church, sealed off certain rooms belonging to the Greek Patriarch and annexed them to the mosque.[17]

Siege of the Church of the Nativity

And then there is the incident and quickly made headlines worldwide: the violation and occupation of the Church of the Nativity. On April 2, 2002, armed Muslim jihadist "militants" fleeing the Israeli army entered the Church of the Nativity, taking Church officials and 200 visitors hostage. During what eventually became a 39-day

---

[13] Sandro Magister, "Custody Must Be Doubled . . ."

[14] "Middle East Christians: Hanna Massd is the pastor of Gaza Baptist Church, one of only three churches serving the 2,000 Christians living among the Gaza Strip's 1.3 million inhabitants," *BBC News,* December 21, 2005.

[15] *The Palestinian Authority's Treatment of Christians in the Autonomous Areas,* Israeli Government report, October 1997; English translation available at http://www.science.co .il/arab-israeli-conflict/ Articles/Imra-1997-10-30.asp.

[16] Yoram Ettinger, "The Islamization of Bethlehem by Arafat," *AP,*

[17] Dore Gold, *The Fight for Jerusalem,* 215.

occupation, the Israelis demonstrated their respect for the shrines of other faiths by refusing to enter the church. The jihadists demonstrated theirs by seizing valuable artifacts and using Bible pages as toilet paper. When they left, agreeing to go into exile, Israeli experts who swept the church found 40 "explosive devices."[18]

As I noted just a moment ago, there is a mosque in Manger Square, so why did the jihadists violate a church? They tore pages out of Bibles and used them for toilet paper – but would not pages from the Koran work just as well? Likewise, as the destruction of Iraq's Golden Mosque demonstrated, jihadists are not shy about blowing up Muslim religious shrines, so why rig the Church of the Nativity with the explosives the Israelis discovered when they were able to gain entry to the church, when a mosque was readily available?

Or how about respecting the sanctity of *all* religious sites and taking your jihad elsewhere?

But the most important aspect of the whole incident was that the international media even reported it at all. For the fact is, Muslim Palestinians habitually and frequently — and deliberately — use Christian sites both as staging areas for attacks on Israel and as sanctuaries afterwards.

Needless to say, when the Israelis finally apprehended the jihadists and sent them into a richly-deserved exile, Christians were not sorry to see them go. "Finally the Christians can breathe freely," said one Christian woman. "We are so delighted that these criminals who have intimidated us for such a long time are now going away."[19]

In other words, thank you, Israel, very much.

---

[18] "Timeline: Bethlehem siege," BBC News, May 10, 2002.
[19] Sayed Anwar, "Exiled Palestinian Militants Ran Two-Year Reign of Terror," *Washington Times*, May 13, 2002.

Property Rights Violations

Christian Palestinians must also live in fear of having their land illegally sold out from under them and, in some cases, seized outright. Here is one way in which a veneer of legality is used to cover what is, in reality, nothing less than outright theft: A Muslim forges a deed to a plot of Christian land and registers it under his name with the Palestinian Authority. A second Muslim then pretends to "illegally seize" the land "registered" by the first one. The first then sues the second to get "his" land back, using the forged documents as "evidence" of ownership. Based on this "evidence" — the forged deed — the court rules for the first Muslim, thus legitimizing validating the fraudulent documents and turning him into the legal owner.

But other actions by the corrupt Palestinian Authority show that the aspiring land-thief need not bother himself with such an elaborate ruse. When a Muslim Palestinian used forged documents to seize the 9,000 square meters of land that Dr. Samir Asfour inherited near the Tomb of Rachel, the register for the district of Bethlehem simply ruled in favor of the Muslim.[20]

Indeed, under the Palestinian Authority's corrupt legal system, even a *favorable* ruling from a Palestinian court does not guarantee justice for Christians in land disputes with Muslims. When a Palestinian court ruled in favor of the Christian Comtsieh family, whose building, in the center of Bethlehem, had been seized by a Muslim family, the PA police simply refused to enforce the verdict. Later, the same judge who initially ruled *for* the Comtsiehs, issued a *second* verdict nullifying the first, effectively awarding ownership to the Muslim family.[21]

---

[20] Sandro Magister, "The Custody Must Be Doubled…"

[21] Danny Naveh (Israeli Minister of Parliamentary Affairs), *The Involvement of Arafat, PA Senior Officials and Apparatuses in Terrorism against Israel, Corruption and Crime,* 2002, http://www.mfa.gov.il/mfa/go.asp?MFAH0lom0.

If the PA merely colluded with land-thieves, that would be bad enough. Unfortunately, sometimes, the land-thief *is* the PA. In January 2007, Fuad Lama, 72, and his wife, Georgette, 69, complained to the PA that "Muslim gangsters" had stolen six dunams (1.5 acres) of their property in Karkafka, just south of Bethlehem. "A lawyer and *an official with the Palestinian Authority* just came and took our land," Georgette said. "We paid them $1,000 so they could help us regain our land. Instead of giving us back our land, they simply decided to keep it for themselves. They even destroyed all the olive trees and divided the land into small plots, apparently so that they could offer each for sale." When Fuad confronted the trespassers, they beat him severely and threatened to shoot him. "My husband is after [sic] heart surgery and they still beat him. These people have no heart. We're afraid to go to our land because they will shoot at us."[22]

The same policies, specifically designed to "legally" deprive Christians of their property, making it hard for many Christians to *keep* their land, also make it extremely difficult for them to *sell* it—that is, to anyone but a Muslim. Christians who have tried to sell their land to other Christians have received death threats. And where Jews are concerned, death is more than just a threat, it's the law: the Palestinian Land Law specifically imposes the death penalty on anyone who sells land to a Jew.[23]

Harassment of Christian Palestinian Women

Christian Palestinian women face the same indignities and assaults as Christian Palestinian men, plus others unique to their sex, including physical abuse up to and including murder, from Muslim Palestinian men who take it

[22] Khaled Abu Tomaeh, "Bethlehem Muslim gang accused of using stolen documents to grab Christians' land," *Jerusalem Post*, April 20, 2007. (emphasis added)
[23] Justus Reid Weiner, 13.

upon themselves to force Christian women to obey the same draconian dress code imposed on Muslim women. A fundamentalist group called The Righteous Swords of Islam, has threatened to behead female television broadcasters who fail to dress in proper Islamic fashion—a threat, given the fates of the Amaro and Amr sisters, female television broadcasters need to take seriously.[24]

If I were one of these female broadcasters, I would take the Righteous Swords' threat seriously. Dressing for the 21st century instead of the seventh earned Sisters Rada and Dunya Amaro death sentences from the Al-Aqsa Martyrs Brigade, who "wanted to clean the Palestinian house of prostitutes"—"prostitutes" being defined as "young, attractive Christian women who wore Western clothes and no veil."[25] Is it any surprise, then, that many Christian women, for their own safety, dress in Islamic garb?[26]

And count the Amr sisters, aged 17 and 19, as two more victims of Muslim Palestinian religious vigilantes. Condemned and summarily executed as "prostitutes," autopsies showed the "prostitutes," in fact, to have been virgins—or at least they were before they were raped by their executioners after having "lit cigarettes applied to their genitals.[27]

Given the fates of the Amaro and Amr sisters, Rawan William, 16, who was gang-raped but not tortured or killed, probably should count herself lucky. *How* lucky, however, is open to question, because of the shame that Arab society attaches to rape victims.

> [T]he attitude towards rape in Middle Eastern
> countries is altogether different from that
> prevalent in the West. . . . [O]nce a girl has been

---

[24] Khaled Abu Toameh, "Gaza 'immodest' women to be killed," *Jerusalem Post*, June 2, 2007.
[25] Elizabeth Day.
[26] Justus Reid Weiner, 15.
[27] Sandro Magister, "The Custody Must Be Doubled..."

raped she is considered "dirty" and unfit for marriage. Therefore, few people are willing to speak out about rape since it is considered so shameful to the victim. Amnesty International ... stated, "In a rape case the onus of proof falls on the victim; moreover, if a woman fails to prove that she did not consent to intercourse the court may convict her of committing *zina* [extramarital relations].[28]

Thus, though many Christians confirm that the rape of Christian women by Muslim men is "widespread" in the Palestinian areas[29] and is "reported to have occurred frequently (especially in Beit Sahur),"[30] the stigma Muslim and Christian society visits on women who publicly acknowledge their violation would seem to indicate that the official figures are low and that we may never know the true figure.

This unfortunate characteristic of pre-modern, traditional Middle Eastern culture, whereby rape makes a woman "'dirty' and unfit for marriage," apparently has fostered a novel tactic: using rape to reduce the Christian population. Call it jihadist birth control. Inaz Muslah, 23, a Christian teacher in Beit Jallah, explains: "Some Muslim guys raped many girls, Christian. And ... she can't [get] married after that. ... People look at her as [a] raped woman. People will talk about her. She can't [get] married after that.[31]

And, in that society, of course, a woman who cannot get married cannot have children.

Forbidden Fruit

The jihadists believe that a Middle East ruled — and ideally, inhabited — exclusively by Muslims, would be Eden.

---

[28] Justus Reid Weiner, 15.
[29] Ibid., 15.
[30] Baruch Kra, "IDF Maintains Cautious Approach to Bethlehem," *Haaretz* (Israel), April 10, 2002. Cited by Raab.
[31] Justus Reid Weiner, 16.

In one way, for Muslim Palestinian men, it already is because, like the Garden of Eden, Judea, Samaria and Gaza contain a forbidden fruit. But is not the one that Eve gave to Adam. For Muslim men, the forbidden fruit is Muslim women. Unable to partake of this forbidden fruit, some Muslim men turn to the only alternative, Christian women. As one Christian man explains, "These Muslim men are preying on Christian girls because they are forbidden from going anywhere near Muslim girls."[32]

Forced Marriage

One of the affronts that turned Iraq's Sunnis against Al Qaeda and inspired the Anbar Awakening, was Al Qaeda's attempts to "arrange" forced marriages between Al Qaeda members and local women.[33] Though our and the Iraqi people's victory has eliminated this practice, and Al Qaeda along with it, forced-marriage fans will be pleased to know that the practice of forced marriages of Christian Palestinian women to Muslim Palestinian men is alive and well in Judea, Samaria and Gaza.

> A relatively poor Muslim family appeared on the doorstep of the home of a wealthy Christian family. The Muslim family brought along a sheikh [clergyman who could perform a Muslim wedding ceremony] and demanded that the Christian daughter, known in both communities for her beauty, wed their son. The father of the Christian family asked for a two-day reprieve to think things over. The Muslim family agreed, but apparently reconsidered, reappearing the following day on the Christian family's doorstep, this time with their son dressed for his

[3232] Matthew Kalman, "Bethlehem's star-crossed lovers," *San Francisco Chronicle*, May 15, 2005.
[33] "Iraqi Sunnis drop al-Qaida over marriages," *UPI*, August 31, 2007. Another reason, of course, is the Sunnis' realizing, finally, that the Americans are liberators, not occupiers.

wedding accompanied by the sheikh and fifteen Muslim men.[34]

Fortunately, this Christian father had two friends of his own: Smith & Wesson. By the time the shooting stopped, three members of the Muslim bridal party lay dead and another ten wounded. The family immediately fled the PA territories, but at least they prevented the marriages. Other Christian parents, less resolute, or at least less well-armed, have acquiesced to the forced marriages of their daughters to Muslim men. "They think the Christians are weak," says George, a Christian Palestinian, "they come with large families and guns and intimidate Christians."[35] "We are afraid," says Mary, who lives in Ramallah. "They have knives [and] guns and can do whatever they want. They can kill you simply . . . [for] speaking bad about them."[36]

Even sympathetic *Muslims* who dare to criticize the treatment of Christians do so at great risk. According to reporter Harry de Quetteville, "Several Christians tell the story of a moderate Muslim imam in Bethlehem's biggest mosque, who was repeatedly threatened after giving a sermon calling for an end to the anti-Christian discrimination and land grabs."[37]

Indifference and Corruption of PA Police and Courts

In any country operating under the rule of law, victims of the kinds of incidents I have described would instinctively turn to the police for protection and to the courts for justice. Unfortunately, as we have seen, at least where Christians (and, I do not doubt, many Muslims) are concerned, Palestinian courts and police are as likely to break the law as to enforce it. What is the point of going to the police when

---

[34] Justus Reid Weiner, 16.
[35] Ibid., 16.
[36] Ibid.
[37] Harry De Quetteville.

the people mistreating you *are* the police? We've already seen the examples of the Armenian gold dealer who was beaten and extorted by the PA police,[38] and the Lamas, whose land was stolen by "an official with the Palestinian Authority."[39] Now here are some more:

- Farid Azizeh, a Christian businessman and former member of the Bethlehem municipal council, used to run a coffee shop in Manger Square. Then he filed a complaint against a Muslim driver who killed two of his relatives in an accident. Refusing to drop the complaint after threats from local Fatah militiamen reputedly recruited by the driver's family, Azizeh was blinded for life when "unidentified gunmen " fired on his car, hitting him in the head. Meanwhile, the "unidentified gunmen" — who, it turns out, are, in reality, eminently identifiable; many Bethlehemites know who they are — remain free.[40]

- Sana Razi Nashash was on her way to complain to the Palestinian Authority police about a man who harassed her the day before. She changed her mind when, on the way, she saw the man — wearing a PA police uniform.[41]

- When a group of Christian men intervened to stop a group of Muslim men from dragging a Christian woman into a car to rape her, the police arrested the *Christians*. The Muslims were not even charged.[42]

- An 18-year-old Muslim Palestinian student murdered a Christian convert's 14-year-old nephew right in front

---

[38] See page 12.
[39] See page 17**Error! Bookmark not defined.**.
[40] Khaled Abu Toameh, "Away from the manger — a Christian-Muslim divide," *Jerusalem Post*, October 21, 2005.
[41] Justus Reid Weiner, 20.
[42] Ibid., 16.

of a teacher. Someone contacted the family to pick up the body; no one bothered to contact the police.[43]

And in the case we mentioned earlier, the gang-rape of 16-year-old Rawan William Mansur,[44] not one of the four perpetrators has been arrested.

"There is no security for us," lamented a Christian Palestinian businessman, after hundreds of rampaging Muslims burned the house and store of a Christian accused of murdering a Muslim man, then torched the man's brother's store, damaged several more Christian businesses and terrorized more than 100 children at youth center. In this case, the question of whether it was worth the bother to call the notoriously corrupt PA police was moot *because they were already there* — and did nothing. "Everyone is taking the law in his own hands. The [accused] man's brother, they burned his house, his shops, his cars and the police of Ramallah *stood by and watched.*"[45]

Even Yasser Arafat's death, welcomed by those of us who are neither Jacques Chirac nor members of the Nobel Peace Prize Committee, was, for Christian Palestinians, a mixed blessing because for them, his successor, the "moderate" Mahmoud Abbas, may be even worse. When the Pope's envoy to Jerusalem presented Arafat with a list of grievances, Arafat responded only with empty promises, but "[a]t least Arafat responded," says Christian television station owner Samir Qumsieh. "Abbas does not answer our letters."[46] When an Italian reporter asked about tensions between Israel and the Vatican, a frustrated Father Pierbattista Pizzabella exploded:

[43] Justus Reid Weiner, 20.
[44] See page **Error! Bookmark not defined.**.
[45] Charles Radin, "Mob Fears Grow in West Bank," *Boston Globe*, February 6, 2002. (emphasis added)
[46] Harry De Quetteville.

What do you mean by difficulties between Israel and the Vatican? We Christians in the Holy Land have other problems. Almost every day— *repeat, almost every day*—our communities are harassed by the Islamic extremists in these regions. And if it's not the members of Hamas or Islamic Jihad, there are clashes with the "rubber wall" of the Palestinian Authority, which does little or nothing to punish those responsible. On occasion, we have even discovered among our attackers the police agents of Mahmoud Abbas or the militants of Fatah, his political party, who are supposed to be defending us.[47]

Christian Omerta

Omerta is the oath Mafia members take not to expose the organization's activities or betray its members. But in Judea, Samaria and Gaza, the Christian Palestinian version of *omerta* requires no oath. Fear suffices:

Out of fear for their safety, Christian spokesmen aren't happy to be identified by name when they complain about the Muslims' treatment of them [but] off the record they talk of harassment and terror tactics, mainly from the gangs of thugs who looted and plundered Christians and their property, *under the protection of Palestinian security personnel.*[48]

A Christian Palestinians using the pseudonym, "Abu Sumayah," agrees. "There is fear. If I lived in London, I would tell you [my real name]. [Here,] somebody will shoot me.[49]

---

[47] Sandro Magister, "Custody Must Be Doubled . . ." (emphasis added)

[48] Hanan Schlein, *Ma'ariv,* December 24, 2001. Translated from Hebrew by Palestinian Media Watch. Cited by Raab. (emphasis added)

[49] Justus Reid Weiner, 23.

Caught in the Crossfire: Christian Palestinian suffering amid Muslim Palestinian "Resistance"

It is unfortunate, but unavoidable, that the security wall Israel built to prevent the infiltration of Muslim Palestinian terrorists and suicide bombers also prevents the free passage of non-jihadist Muslims. That is indeed unfortunate, but it is also a fact that many Muslim Palestinians, while not actively participating in the anti-Israel jihad, nevertheless support it, and demonstrated that support by voting in large numbers for Hamas in the 1996 election that brought the marginally-more-terrorist-than-Fatah gang to power.

No, the greater injustice, by far, is the suffering of *Christian* Palestinians, those unfortunate enough to find themselves on the wrong side of the security wall. Unlike the Muslim Palestinians, who voted overwhelmingly for Hamas, a poll of Christian Palestinians, taken during the run-up to the 1996 election, failed to find a single Christian who intended to vote for either Hamas or the other slightly-more-terrorist-than-Fatah party, Islamic Jihad.[50]

And of course, *there are no Christian suicide bombers.*[51] Christians literally, and unfairly, are caught in the crossfire of a "resistance" for which they bear no responsibility and of which they want no part.

Worse, it is a crossfire into which the Muslim Palestinians have *deliberately* put them, by *deliberately*, attacking from, and fleeing into, Christian areas so as to draw retaliatory fire onto the Christians,[52] for the twin purposes of drawing such

---

[50] Bernard Sabella, Middle East Study Association Annual Meeting, San Francisco, November 2001.

[51] Actually, there is one single case of a suicide bomber, Loula Abboud, but she was Lebanese. (United Nations, *Department for Disarmament Affairs Panel Discussion on Making Disarmament More Effective: Men and Women Working Together*, April 15 2003. It should also be noted that George Habash, founder and leader of the Popular Front for the Liberation of Palestine, "whose terror specialties included airplane hijacking, hostage taking, massacre, assassination, and suicide bombings," was a Christian. (Caroline Glick, "Our World: Habash's last laugh," *Jerusalem Post*, February 4, 2008. However, these are very much exceptions that prove the rule that Christian terrorism is more than sufficiently rare to justifiably characterize Christian Palestinians (remember, the Christian suicide bomber was Lebanese, not Palestinian) as nonviolent.

[52] Heather Sharp, "Holy Land Christians' decline," *BBC News Website*, December 15, 2005, http://news.bbc.co.uk/1/hi/world/middle_east/4514254.stm.

fire *away* from Muslim Palestinian neighborhoods, and making Christian Palestinians unwilling participants in, and victims of a murderous cause of which, again, Christian Palestinians want no part. Indeed, Elizabeth Day, of England's *Daily Mail*, reports that, "in 2004, half of the Israeli fatalities caused by Muslim Palestinian attacks originated in Bethlehem."[53] And in September 2000, the Palestinian Tanzim militia deliberately chose the Christian town of Beit Jala to set up sniper posts from which to shoot at civilians in Jerusalem, even though there were alternative, Muslim, sites within rifle range of Jewish settlements in Judea or Samaria.

Indeed, in Beit Jala, Muslim Palestinian snipers made a point of positioning themselves near Christian homes, churches and hotels specifically to invite an Israeli response and "knowing that a slight deviation in Israeli return fire would harm Christian institutions or homes." [54] The object, of course, is to provide Western media with stories and images of suffering Christians, which the jihadists and their anti-Semitic sympathizers at the BBC[55] can then use to indict Israel for the "crime" of defending herself and, ideally, drive a wedge between Israel and her Christian friends and supporters.

Not only do Muslim Palestinian jihadists feel neither guilt nor regret about drawing Christians, unwillingly, into the Muslim Palestinian's anti-Israel jihad, they believe it only *right and fair* to force Christian Palestinians to sacrifice themselves and their children to the "resistance." A "prominent Evangelical pastor with influential contacts in

---

[53] Elizabeth Day.
[54] Yoram Ettinger, cited by Raab.
[55] See the Web site of HonestReportingUK for an analysis, including examples, of BBC anti-Israel/Semitic reporting in 2007, http://www.honestreporting.co.uk/articles/critiques/One_Year_Analysis_The_BBC_in_2007.asp. To cite just one, "60% of articles about Israeli operations [in Judea, Samaria and Gaza] named Israel or the [Israel Defense Forces] directly as the perpetrator [("Israelis kill militants in Gaza," "Children killed in Israeli strike")] while only 15% of stories about Palestinian violence named the perpetrators [(typical headlines for stories on violence perpetrated by Muslim Palestinians: "Rocket injures dozens in Israel," "West Bank clash leaves three dead."].

the West Bank" explains: "[N]o Christian blood has been spilled [in the Muslim Palestinian "resistance"], only Muslim blood . . . Muslims have donated their children to the cause, but Christians haven't."[56]

In other words, if Christian Palestinians will not voluntarily spill their blood in the Muslim Palestinians' cause, Muslim Palestinians will spill it *for* them.

"Hamastan"

After seizing control of Gaza from Fatah, Hamas wasted no time in making clear its intention to turn the Gaza Strip into an Islamic theocracy," a virtual "Hamastan." Just two days after Muslims attacked a church and a Christian school, Sheik Abu Saqer, a "militant leader" of "Islamic outreach" movement Jihadia Salafiya, announced:

> I expect our Christian neighbors to understand the new Hamas rule means real changes. *They must be ready for Islamic rule* if they want to live in peace in Gaza.
>
> Jihadia Salafiya and other Islamic movements will ensure Christian schools show publicly what they are teaching to be sure they are not carrying out missionary activity. No more alcohol on the streets. All women, including non-Muslims, need to understand they must be covered at all times while in public.
>
> Also the activities of Internet cafes, pool halls and bars must be stopped. If it goes on, we'll attack these things very harshly.

Accusing "the leadership of the Gaza Christian community of 'proselytizing and trying to convert Muslims

---

[56] Justus Reid Weiner, "The Use of Palestinian Children in the Al-Aqsa Intifada: A Legal and Political Analysis," 16 *Temp. Int'L & Comp. L.J.* 43. Cited by Justus Reid Weiner in Justus Reid Weiner, *Human Rights of Christians in Palestinian Society*.

with funding from American evangelicals," Abu Saqer warned that "[t]his missionary activity is endangering the entire Christian community in Gaza" and vowed that "missionary activity" will be "dealt with harshly."[57]

Gaza: Christians Attacked

Here is what life is like for Christians in "Hamastan":

September 25, 2007, A "masked man dressed in black" assaults Claire Farah Tarazi, an 80-year-old Christian Gazan, in her own home:

> "He was carrying a club and a sharp tool," she said. "As soon as I opened the door, he pushed me inside and shouted: 'Where is the money, you infidel?' I shouted back: "I'm not an infidel — I'm a proud Palestinian Arab."
>
> Tarazi said the assailant had beaten her on the hand with the club, demanding that she hand over all her money and jewelry.
>
> "I was so terrified that I gave him two golden bracelets, a cell phone and a few hundred shekels," she said. "But the man said this was not enough and hit me hard on the head with a tool he was carrying until I started bleeding." He then locked her in her bedroom and started searching the house for money and valuable items.

Tarazi's relatives have no doubt that she was attacked because of her faith. As one relative said, "The fact that the attacker called her an infidel speaks for itself."[58]

October 7, 2007: 32-year old Christian Palestinian Rami Khader Ayyad, director of the Gaza Strip's only Christian

[57] Aaron Klein, "Christians must accept Islamic rule," *ynet news.com*, June 19, 2007. Originally reported on World Net Daily. Available online at http://www .ynetnews.com/articles/0,7340,L-3414753,00.html.
[58] Khaled Abu Toameh, "Gaza: Christian-Muslim tensions heat up," *Jerusalem Post*, September 25, 2007.

bookstore is murdered, sending "a shudder of fear through the Gaza Strip's tiny Christian community, which is feeling increasingly insecure since the Islamic Hamas seized control there last summer. . . ." This same Christian bookstore that was been firebombed in April. Ayyad leaves behind two young children and a pregnant wife.

February 15, 2008: "A band of 14 masked gunmen" invade the YMCA library, planting explosives that destroy "thousands of books." A second "explosive device" planted near a computer, fails to detonate.[59]

Lebanon

It is no accident that the non-Jewish Middle Eastern state in which Christians enjoy the most rights, the most prosperity and the most freedom from persecution, Lebanon, also has the largest Christian population relative to Muslims. As must be apparent to even the casual observer, in any country where Christians and Muslims live together, Christian fortunes very much depend on the Christians being not just the majority, but the overwhelming majority.[60] Unfortunately,   collaboration   by   Muslim   Lebanese, Hezbollah (many of whom are not Lebanese), and dhimmi Christians with Syria is causing the same rapid diminution of the Christian population that we see in Judea, Samaria

---

[59] "Gunmen explode YMCA library in Gaza," *Jerusalem Post*, February 15, 2008.

[60] As a demonstration of this point, this writer, using Google, compiled a rough list of countries arranging them in rough order of the militancy of the Muslim population (so that, for example, countries such as England, where Muslim militancy clearly is becoming increasingly a problem, would be ahead of countries such as the United States, where it is not. As the result of this admittedly rudimentary research, I have pegged the "magic number" at roughly 3 percent: As the Muslim percentage of a country's population approaches 3 percent, the Muslim community becomes more assertive, enclaves begin to form and as the 3 percent threshold is passed, Muslim militancy becomes a problem. Indeed, in my country, the United States, from childhood well into adulthood (I was born in 1952), my only exposure to Islam was through *The Arabian Nights* and Hollywood movies. To cite just a few examples of how assertive and "in-your-face" Islam has become, today, in my home state of Michigan, the city of Dearborn, once considered an elitist "white enclave" is now so heavily Muslim that it has been nicknamed "Dearbornistan;" Hamtramck, once a Polish (and Catholic) enclave, not only contains mosques, but Muslims recently sued for — and won — the right to broadcast, *through loudspeakers*, the muezzins' five-times-daily call to prayer; Muslim taxi drivers in Minneapolis use public restrooms at the airport to wash their feet before prayers; Muslim college students do the same in campus restrooms and at least one university is installing footbaths; Muslim college students have commandeered some campus meditation rooms, turning them into virtual mosques, complete with male-female separation barriers; Muslims have been seen to lay out prayer rugs and pray publicly at baseball games.

and Gaza. With shocking speed, what was once a secure majority is being transformed into an insecure minority:

> Lebanon [is a revealing case] precisely because no one, a generation or two ago, would have imagined that their large historic Christian communities would be so beleaguered today. And yet they are. [W]here Christians were once a solid majority of the country, they number less than one million people [as of December 2001], and are shrinking rapidly.[61]

History of Lebanese Christendom

To appreciate the plight of Lebanon's Christians in the present, we must know something of their past. Lebanon's major Christian sect, the Maronites, trace their history back to a St. John Maro, who, if he actually existed,[62] would have lived in the seventh century. Others say that the name, "Maronite," comes from the sixth century convent of Beit-Marun.[63]

But when and how the Maronites' began is less important than where they lived, and still do: a lucky accident of geography known as Mount Lebanon. Contrary to what its name would imply, Mount Lebanon is not a single mountain, but an entire range of them, running parallel to the Mediterranean coast, rising as high as 3,088 feet above sea level. This forbidding terrain acted as a natural barrier against foreign invasion and allowed the Maronites to do, for centuries, what no other non-Muslims in Arabia could: resist Muslim conquest and subjugation. As the Muslim conquests swallowed up civilization after civilization— Egyptian, Assyrian, Persian, Byzantine, Indian, and others—

[61] Adelman and Kuperman.
[62] Sadly, the definitive story of the Maronites' origin has been lost. Historians agree only back to the 16th century, by which time the Maronites were already established and had been for centuries.
[63] *Maronites*, Catholic Encyclopedia, http://newadvent.org/cathen/09683c.htm.

(mis)appropriating them under the rubric of a mythical "golden age" of Islamic civilization, the Maronites survived, generation after generation, eventually coming to co-rule, with the Druze (a small Muslim sect), an "autonomous principality" that endured until the dissolution of the Ottoman Empire in the aftermath of the First World War.[64]

The Ottomans' decision to side with Germany in that war proved disastrous. What had been a vast Muslim empire was reduced by the victorious allies, England and France, to a single state, Turkey, with the remainder divided between England and France and administered by them under a mandate from the newly-formed League of Nations.[65] The arrangement was concluded in the spring of 1920, in the town of San Remo, Italy.

As soon as the ink dried on the San Remo Agreement, the two European countries proceeded to carve up their portions. Unfortunately, they did this with little regard to the history, religion, traditions and ethnicity of the people who would actually be living in the states they were creating out of thin air.[66] The result, not unexpectedly, was a motley conglomeration of artificial states, with artificial borders and, most important, artificial nationalities.

Subsequent history would quickly prove the folly of that approach.   Creating a *nation* is one thing; creating the *nationalities* to go along with it is quite another, especially when most of the people expected to comprise those nationalities never sought independence in the first place. As far as the Muslims were concerned, they already *had* their own state: the Ottoman Empire, of which every Muslim was a subject. Consequently, when France tried to consult with

[64] Ibid.
[65] Kamal Salibi, *A House of Many Mansions: The History of Lebanon Reconsidered* (I.B taauris & Co., Ltd.: 1993), 19-37.
[66] And they dare to criticize *my* countries occasional (and reluctantly admitted) ham-handed foreign policy. How does one say "chutzpah" in French?

the Muslims on what kind of states they wanted, the Muslims, could not articulate any coherent vision for the "new" Middle East. Which was understandable, since they were perfectly content with the "old" Middle East.

But the Christians could.[67] After centuries of fending off Muslim attempts to subjugate them, Christians knew exactly what they wanted: self-determination, in their own, Christian, state. They also had the good fortune to have sided with the victors in the War, and, in return for that support, were entitled to some deference to their aspirations. Conversely, to the Muslims, who supported Germany, the Allies owed nothing.

The Christians took full advantage of their moral entitlement, and then some, in an exercise in hubris that, in time—our time—would prove fatal. Not content to limit the area of their new state to their traditional Mount Lebanon homeland, the Christians overreached, asking a substantial chunk of *Muslim* land as well, to create a "Greater Lebanon" stretching from Tripoli, Beirut, Sidon and Tyre on the Mediterranean coast, to the Bekaa Valley in the east.

Understandably, the idea of a "Greater Lebanon" did not sound so "great" to the Muslims living in these Muslim areas, who were converted, overnight, from the majority in a Muslim state, to a minority in a Christian one.   Islam's traditional view of Christians as inferiors, and the Koran's dictum that only Muslims may rule over Muslims, only made their humiliation worse.[68] Today, we can only speculate on how different, and peaceful, Lebanon might be had the Maronites restrained themselves and limited their demands to their traditional enclaves.[69]

---

[67] And of course, so could the Jews. But this book is about Christians and anyway, the Jews' story—Zionism, the Balfour Declaration, etc.—is well known.

[68] Kamal Salibi.

[69] The difference between what the Christians did, and what the Jewish Palestinians were to do a generation later ould not be more stark: Whereas the Maronites asked for more than their traditional homeland, the Jewish Palestinians, in accepting the 1947 partition, settled for much less. A map of the

Which is not to say that we cannot assign to others a share of the blame. The French, for one, probably should have known better than to give in to the Maronites' demands, but the Muslims deserve their share of blame, too, since what *they* wanted—restoration of the Ottoman Empire—was unattainable and they failed to advance any alternative proposal, leaving the French to muddle through the best they could, on their own.

And muddle they did, creating not one, not two, but *four* Muslim states, with no overarching logic for either number or nature, Two of them, the States of Aleppo and Damascus, were geography; the other two, the States of the Alouites and of the Jebel Druze, were based on ethnicity and religion.[70] Not surprisingly and probably inevitably, the four Muslim states soon merged into just one: Syria.

That left Lebanon—officially Christian, but in Muslim eyes rightfully Muslim and rightfully part of Syria. As far as Muslims were concerned, the Maronites "had no right securing for their Greater Lebanon Syrian territory which had once belonged to Damascus."[71] So if you've been wondering why Syria occupied Lebanon for decades and why she constantly meddles in Lebanon's affairs, now you know: Syria has never accepted Lebanon's independence, viewing her the same way China views Taiwan, as a "renegade province" that should—and absent the interference of outside powers, would—be part of the "mother country."

The Maronites nevertheless should at least have foreseen the potential for tension with the new Muslim minority of their "Greater Lebanon," if not that the Muslims' higher

---

original UN-proposed partition can be viewed at http://en.wikipedia.org/wiki/Image:1947-UN-Partition-Plan-1949-ArmisticeComparison.png. Note the gerrymandered configuration and Jerusalem's proposed status as an "international" city, with neither Jews nor Christians exercising sovereignty over the entire area.
[70] Kamal Salibi.
[71] Ibid.

birthrate might someday change that minority into a majority. Sensitivity and, where possible, accommodation to Muslim sensitivities should have been the order of the day. Instead, the Christians proceeded to treat Muslims with an *in*sensitivity that could not help but antagonize them. For example, however understandable it may have been for the Maronites to fight alongside France in her campaign to crush the Meccan emir's son, King Feisal, who was trying to establish his own "Syrian empire," there was no need to rub salt in the wound by openly celebrating Feisal's defeat. Add in the tendency of Christian Lebanese, like Christian Palestinians and Christian Egyptians, tended to be more worldly and affluent than their Muslim neighbors, and the Maronites' determination to control the government and to prevent the Muslims from co-governing as political equals,[72] and one has to wonder how such a cauldron of grievances could *not* lead to civil war.

And so civil war came, in 1975. The following year, Christians formed an autonomous enclave north of Beirut that, at first, thanks to Mount Lebanon's forbidding geography, was able to resist "the onslaught of 35,000 Syrian troops and their allied Islamist militias," as their ancestors had resisted the Ottomans in earlier times. But not for long. Unfortunately, as the Syrians learned from Israel on the Golan Heights, and the Taliban learned from us in Afghanistan, mountains no longer offer the same kind of protection against modern armies that they once formed against ancient ones.

By 1990, it was all over for the Lebanon's Christians.[73] From there, matters could only got worse.

---

[72] Ibid. Regarding "Syrian empire," see Efraim Karsh, *Islamic Imperialism*, 137-138.
[73] Walid Phares, referencing his own book "At-Ta'addudiya fi Lubnan (Junieh: Kasleek University Press, 1979), 207-334.

Enter the Syrians

For Syria, Lebanon's civil war Syria's golden opportunity to avenge—and ideally, reverse—the Maronites' 1920 "declaration of independence." Christians suffered grievously at the hands of the Syrians and their Muslim Lebanese allies as "dozens of Christian villages and towns ... were attacked, razed, and ethnically cleansed. ... Massive Syrian bombardments of the Christian areas left thousands of casualties."[74]

After 15 years of resistance, Christian power—and autonomy—were broken in Lebanon.[75] Syria, now in complete control, toppled Lebanon's constitutional government and replaced it with a puppet regime, which it then proceeded to infiltrate with Syrian spies.[76]

The result of Syria's rape of Lebanon is there for all to see, whenever a car bomb explodes, and another Lebanese patriot is assassinated: "an environment virtually uninhabitable for decent people."[77]

Especially Christians.

"Systematic Persecution"

The end of the Lebanese civil war marked the beginning of a campaign of "systematic persecution" of Christians, including arrests and torture of Christian journalists, students and activists and the imposition of restrictive immigration policies,[78] all intended to reduce both the Christians' political power and their physical numbers. For example, all Muslims displaced during the civil war were allowed to return to their homes, but most Christians were not.[79] A naturalization decree, passed in 1994, increased the

---

[74] Walid Phares, "Are Christian Enclaves the Solution?", *Middle East Quarterly*, Winter 2001, available online at http://www.meforum.org/article/18.
[75] Ibid.
[76] Ibid.
[77] William W. Harris, *The New Face of Lebanon: History's Revenge*, (Princeton: Markus Wiener Publishers, 2005), 314.
[78] Walid Phares, "Are Christian Enclaves the Solution?"
[79] Ibid.

Lebanese population by 10 percent; 80 percent of these new citizens were Muslim.[80] The result, as predictable as it was deliberate, was a "weakening [of] the Christian voice in Lebanon."[81]

To achieve this massive, and speedy, influx of Muslim immigrants, the Lebanese government stopped treating each immigration request individually[82] as it was required to do by the 1989 "Ta'if Agreement." And the betrayal did not stop there.

Named after the Saudi city in which it was signed, the Ta'if Agreement was intended to reconcile the Christian and Muslim communities after 15 years of civil war. Instead, Ta'if became a way for Muslim Lebanese and their Syrian patrons to diminish the Christians' numbers, influence, political power and, ultimately, legal rights by altering Lebanon's unique system of power-sharing, a key source of Lebanese political stability. Under the Lebanese political system, the president is always a Maronite; the premier, a Sunni Muslim and the speaker of the legislature, a Shiite. Though Ta'if appeared to preserve this tradition, it actually altered the distribution of power in a way that greatly increased the power of the Muslim prime minister and speaker at the expense of that of the Christian president.[83] An electoral law, enacted in 1992, led to a gerrymandering of electoral districts so detrimental to Christians that Muslims routinely elected Christian legislators who did not represent the view of most Christians. Indeed, in the 1992 election, the first one held after the end of the civil war, 35 percent of Christian deputies (legislators) were in fact elected by

---

[80] Al-Jarida ar-Rasmiya, Official Gazette, June 03, 1994; Ash-Sharq al-Awsat, November 11, 1998. Cited by Farid el Khazen, "Lebanon — Independent No More," Middle East Quarterly, Winter 2001.
[81] Edward Yeranian, "Christians in Lebanon See Hopes, Numbers Diminish," Christian Science Monitor, May 9, 1997.
[82] Waddah Sharara, Dawlat Hizbullah. Lubnan Mujtama'an Islamiyan (Beirut: Dar an-Nahar, September 27, 1997. Cited by Farid el Khazen.
[83] Joseph Maila, The Document of National Understanding: A Commentary (Oxford: Centre for Lebanese Studies, 1992), 1-62. Cited by Farid el Khazen.

Muslims.[84] As one Lebanese cardinal put it, "Just because you have a [specific number] of people from different sects doesn't mean the government is representative."[85] American University of Beirut Professor Farid el Khazen was even more blunt: "[Lebanese] Christians today are not in a position to veto government decisions, nor alter policies detrimental to their political and communal interests."[86]

Finally, there was the physical presence, until recently, of tens of thousands of Syrian soldiers, another "benefit" of the Ta'if Agreement. It is no exaggeration to say, as former Lebanese parliament member Albert Moukheiber did, that "for all practical purposes, [the Ta'if Agreement] gave up all sovereignty to Syria."[87]

Lebanon Today

"Lebanon today is not a reassuring place for Christians," writes journalist Elizabeth Picard.[88] A major reason why is the rise of Islamic extremism and Hezbollah. As Lebanon's Muslim population grows larger, it grows increasingly radical, causing Christians to leave at an increasing rate, which in turn increases the rate of Muslim radicalization, which in turn forces out more Christians, and so on, and so on:

> "Some 60,000-70,000 Christians have left the country in the last six months," said George Khoury, executive director of Caritas Lebanon [a Catholic relief agency]. . . . Lebanon is becoming increasingly Islamized because of the demographic shift."

[84] Farid el Khazen, *Lebanon's First Postwar Parliamentary Election: An Imposed Choice* (Oxford: Centre for Lebanese Studies, 1998), 27.
[85] Edward Yeranian.
[86] Farid el Khazen, *Lebanon's First Postwar . . .*
[87] Quoted in Edward Yeranian.
[88] Elizabeth Picard, "The Dynamics of the Lebanese Christians: From the Paradigm of the 'Ammiyyat to the Paradigm of Hwayyek," *Christians Communities in the Arab Middle East. The Challenge of the Future,* ed. Andrea Pacini (Oxford: Clarendon Press, 1998), 200-221. Cited by Farid el Khazen, "Lebanon — Independent No More,"

Jawad Adra, managing partner of Information International, warned that the increasing polarization of Lebanon's pro- and anti-government factions was providing a fertile breeding ground for Sunni extremism, which is only likely to hasten the pace of Christian emigration from the country.

"The growth of Sunni extremism is a ticking time bomb that is waiting to explode and could sweep all moderates out of its path," he said.[89]

I don't have my finger on the pulse of Lebanese Sunni extremism, but Hezbollah's recent (mid-2008) hijacking of the Lebanese government demonstrates clearly that in terms of Lebanon's Shiites, Adra's prediction, made little more than a year before, has come true.

Another of Adra's "time bombs" could, perhaps, be thought of as a secondary explosion touched off by the notorious "Danish cartoon incident." To show their offense—and a serious lack of both a sense of humor and sense of self-esteem—at a series of *cartoons*, 20,000 angry Muslim Lebanese torched the Danish embassy. Then they turned their rage on the Beirut Christian community, killing one Christian and wounding 28:

Waving green Islamic flags and chanting "God is greatest," they also threw stones at the Maronite Catholic church as violent protests spread towards Christian areas in eastern Beirut. ... [T]he protestors attacked properties and ships in ... the Christian area of Ashrafiyeh, throwing stones, breaking windows and overturning cars, eyewitnesses said.

---

[89] Michael Hirst, "Christians flee Lebanon amid signs of growing Islamic fundamentalism, study says," *Catholic News Service*, April 18, 2007. (emphasis added)

Some were seen carrying banners that read "Whoever insults Prophet Mohammed is to be killed."[90]

"Lebanon has always been a bastion of religious tolerance," says Father Samir Samir, "but now it is moving towards the model of Islamization seen in Iraq and Egypt."[91]

Christians in the Crossfire

The Muslim Palestinian tactic I described earlier, of attacking Israel from Christian areas,[92] has spread to Lebanon, where "Hezbollah is using Christian villages to shield its military operations against Israel." During the 2006 Hezbollah-Israel war, says one Christian, "Southern Lebanese Christian villages ... [were] being used by Hezbollah terrorists for launching missile attacks," an account confirmed by a Lebanese military officer, Col. Charbel Barkat, who says "Hezbollah [was] hiding among civilian populations and launching attacks behind human shields."[93] In the 2006 Lebanon war, Israeli jets demolished a Christian man's house after Hezbollah fighters launched a salvo of Katyusha rockets from his roof — with the man's family inside. When family members fled the wreckage, Hezbollah fighters fired on several of them, wounding two.[94]

Discrimination in Public Services and Business

So weak is the Lebanese government that, in the south, for all practical purposes, Hezbollah rules — and the rules are much more favorable to Muslims than to Christians. Christians pay taxes for services that rarely are provided,

---

[90] Stefan J. Bos, "Lebanon Christians Attacked, Church Stoned, By Angry Muslims," *BosNewsLife*, February 6, 2006. http://www.christianpersecution .info.

[91] Michael Hirst, "Rise in radical Islam last straw for Lebanon's Christians," *Sunday Telegraph* (London), April 12, 2007.

[92] See page 26.

[93] Rev. Dr. Keith Roderick, "Hezbollah is using Christian Villages to Shield its Military Operations in Violation of International Law," *Coalition for Responsible Peace in the Middle East*, July 2006. Available online at http://c4rpme.org/bin/articles.cgi?Cat =Christians&Subcat=cmr&ID-510.

[94] Rev. Dr. Keith Roderick.

while Muslims pay no taxes for services that are.[95] In my opinion, no one should be surprised to see the same thing happen in the north, now that Hezbollah has commandeered the entire country.

Muslim Lebanese, like their Palestinian counterparts, boycott Christian businesses. Elias, a farmer in South Lebanon, may have no choice but to sell the land that has belonged to his family for more than a thousand years because, "No one wants to buy the produce from our land as we are Christians and the Muslim community is so strong. *I think that, probably after 10 or 15 years there will be no Christians in Lebanon.*"[96]

New Threats – Bombings

In recent years, Muslims extremists have increasingly turned to bombing to terrorize the Christian population. In September 2005, "a car bomb exploded in a mainly Christian residential neighborhood" in Beirut, killing one person and wounding 20.[97]

In February 2007, three "bombs packed with metal pellets exploded "in the mainly Christian area of Lebanon," killing three and wounding "more than 20."[98]

In May 2007, a bomb exploded near a Christian radio station, killing one and wounding seven.[99] Later that same month, a woman was killed in an explosion near a Beirut shopping mall.[100]

[95] Ibid.
[96] "Lebanese Christians: Elias," *BBC News*, December 28, 2005, http://news.bbc.co.uk /2/hi/ Americas/4506452.stm. (emphasis added)
[97] "Christian Area in Lebanon Bombed
[98] Daniel Blake, "Lebanon Bomb Attacks Bring Destruction to Christian Area," *Christian Today*, February 14,   2007,   http://www.christiantoday.com/article/Lebanon   .bomb.attacks .bring.destruction.to.christian.area/9537.htm
[99] "Bomb in Christian area of Lebanon," *BBC News*, May 7, 2005, http://news.bbc.co.uk /2/hi/ middle_east/4523903.stm.
[100] "Woman reported killed in explosion at mall in East Beirut," *AP*, May 21, 2007.

In June 2007, "A bomb exploded in an empty passenger bus parked in a Christian neighborhood east of Beirut . . . injuring 10 passers-by."[101]

Also in June 2007, An explosion near the Christian town of Jounieh set off "large fires in several buildings."[102]

Political Assassinations

Bombs also appear to be the weapon of choice in a wave of assassinations of Christian anti-Syrian politicians and journalists.

September 2005, "May Chidiac, a news anchor for the Christian-owned Lebanese Broadcasting Corporation, had an arm and leg amputated, thanks to a bomb "planted under the driver's seat of her Range Rover."

June 2005: "Samir Kassir, a [Christian] columnist with the anti-government An-Nahar newspaper, was torn in half by a bomb placed under the seat of his car . . ."[103]

December 2005, Christian "Journalist and lawmaker Gibran Tueni, a relentless critic of Syria who spent months in France fearing assassination, was killed . . . in a car bombing."[104]

November 21, 2006, Pierre Gemayel, is assassinated.[105]

September 19, 2007, Christian parliamentarian Antoine Ghanem is killed in a bombing in the Christian Sin el-Fil district, along with six others."[106]

Egypt

Most Christian Egyptians follow the Coptic Orthodox faith.[107] Descendants of the ancient Egyptians, with a 5,000-

[101] "Loud explosion rocks east Beirut neighborhood," *AP*, June 4, 2007, http://www.iht.com/articles/ap/2007/06/04/africa/ME-GEN-Lebanon-Explosion.php.
[102] "Bomb Explosion Rocks Beirut," *AP*, June 7, 2007, http://cbs2chicago.com/topstories/topstories_story_158155516.html.
[103] Mitchell Prothero, "Anti-Syrian columnist killed in explosion," *The Washington Times*, June 3, 2005.
[104] "Bomb Kills Anti-Syrian In Lebanon," *AP*, December 12, 2005, http://www.cbsnews.com/stories/2005/12/12/world/main1116177.shtml
[105] *Daily Star* online edition staff, "Pierre Gemayel's assassination," *The Daily Star* (Lebanon), November 21, 2006, http://www.dailystar.com.lb/article.asp?edition_id =1&categ_id=2&article_id=77064
[106] Yoav Stern, "Anti-Syrian MP, 6 others killed in Beirut car bomb," *Haaretz* (Israel), September 16 2007.

year history, Copts are a direct link to Egypt's glorious past.[108] Indeed, the name, Copt, is derived from the Arabic *qubt*, which, in turn, comes from the Greek word for Egyptian.[109]

Today, they are the largest Christian population of any Middle Eastern country,[110] though precisely how many Christians there are in Egypt is hard to ascertain. In 2005, the Egyptian government cited an official figure of 5.6 million, but the Egyptian church puts the number much higher, at 11 million, a figure that cannot be verified because the Egyptian government forbids the Egyptian church to conduct an official census.[111]

Egypt was one of the first lands beyond Palestine to be Christianized, by St. Mark, who arrived in the first century. When the Muslim conquests reached Egypt, in 641, Christians were the overwhelming majority—and on the cusp of precipitous decline as Egypt's Muslim conquerors began "a centuries-long process of ethnic and cultural assimilation, conversion, intermarriage, and absorption of large segments of the Egyptian population into the Arab-Islamic culture."[112] Unlike St. Mark, who was able to convert an entire nation with just his word, Islam, as it has throughout its history, needed the sword.

Caught "between desert and Nile,"[113] without the benefit of the kind of mountainous terrain that enabled the Lebanese Maronites to hold out for centuries, Egypt's Christians were quickly reduced to second-class status,[114]

[107] Imad Boles, "Egypt—Persecution: Disappearing Christians of the Middle East," *Middle East Quarterly*, Winter 2001.
[108] "History of the Copts," *U.S. Copts Association*, http://www.copts.com/English/HistoryOfCopts.aspx.
[109] "Coptic Church," Country Studies, *U.S. Library of Congress*. Available online at http://www.countrystudies.us/Egypt/70.htm.
[110] Walid Phares, "Are Christian Enclaves the Solution?"
[111] *Egypt*, Christian Solidarity Worldwide Web site, http://www.cswusa.com /Countries/Egypt.htm
[112] U.S. Copts Association.
[113] Walid Phares, "Are Christian Enclaves the Solution?"
[114] Imad Boles.

and their numbers sharply reduced. At the dawn of the 641 Muslim invasion there were 2.5 million Copts in Egypt.[115] By the end of the 19th century, only 300,000 were left.[116]

During the centuries of Muslim domination, the pendulum of the Copts' treatment, and mistreatment swung from repression to tolerance, and back again more than once. For example, in 1855, the jizya was lifted and Copts also were allowed to join the army. In the following year, the Sultan, 'Abd al-Majid, declared all Ottoman subjects equal before the law, regardless of faith.[117] Muslims and Christians also "worked side by side with Muslims in opposition to British occupation and did, in fact, enjoy rights of citizenship that came close to their Muslim counterparts."[118]

But not equal. At no time have Egypt's Christians enjoyed full equality with Muslims and however much their situation might improve, the improvement would prove to be only temporary as, inevitably, the pendulum swung back, bringing a return to intolerance with it. Sometimes, repressive policies would be instituted with the full knowledge and even participation of the very same British authorities against whom Muslims and Christians had, in earlier times, been united. For example, to appease the Muslim masses, who did not share the government's enlightened views,[119] Sir Eldon Gorst, British high commissioner from 1907 to 1911, "introduced a system that effectively barred Copts from senior government positions.[120] When, in 1911, the Copts specifically demanded full equality with Muslims, those demands "fell on deaf

---

[115] Hilal Khashan.

[116] Walid Phares, "Are Christian Enclaves the Solution?"

[117] Imad Boles.

[118] Saad Eddin Ibrahim, "Christians Oppressed," *Wall Street Journal*, November 18, 2005.

[119] In fairness, it would be unfair to assign all the blame for Muslim intolerance on the Ottomans, who, as the examples I just gave indicate, realized full well that the Eastern, Islamic civilization was losing ground to the West and that Muslim intolerance was a major factor in the East's decline. Most of the blame belongs to the Muslim "man on the street," who resisted, often violently, any attempt by the Ottoman government to grant equality to non-Muslims.

[120] Imad Boles.

Muslim ears"[121]—and on deaf British ears—as both the British occupation and the Muslim majority dismissed the Copts' grievances as "fabricated."[122]

Which, in fairness, is not to say that all Muslims participated in the repression of their non-Muslim minorities. In the mid-19th century, Muslim reformers, such as Muhammad Abduh, tried to "modernize" Islam by "allowing the introduction of Western ideas and by applying reason to religious revelation"[123] Then, as now, the reformers' efforts were thwarted by conservative opposition and the growing movement toward Islamic fundamentalism. Egypt's Copts, like all infidels, including Jews, and Baha'is, were swept up by this movement and the imposition of ancient Shari'a law that accompanied it.

Aside from its immediate effect on non-Muslim Egyptians, the rise of Egyptian Islamic fundamentalism in the mid-19th century came, in time, to affect—and threaten— the entire world because it led to the founding of the Muslim Brotherhood, to which many of today's major jihadist movements, such as Al Qaeda, Hamas and Hezbollah, trace their roots. Critics, skeptics and haters of George Bush delude themselves in thinking our fight is only with Al Qaeda. Everyone needs to understand the Muslim Brotherhood's role as progenitor and lodestar of the modern Islamofascism movement.[124] For example, Osama Bin

---

[121] Hilal Khashan.

[122] *Report by the Heliopolis Congress Organizing Committee,* quoted in Barbara L. Carter, *The Copts in Egyptian Politics: 1918-1952* (Cairo: The American University in Cairo Press, 1986), 9; quoted in turn, by Imad Boles.

[123] Donald Malcolm Reid, "Muhammad Abduh," *Encyclopedia of Politics and Religion,* Robert Wuthnow, ed. (Washington, D.C.: Congressional Quarterly, 1998), 537.
By the way, does Abduh's desire to integrate reason into Islam sound familiar? It was precisely on this point, when Pope Benedict XVI, merely quoted a 14th century Byzantine emperor's comment, to an educated Persian, regarding the role—or non-role—of reason in Islam, that angry Muslim masses rioted all over the world (and, by rioting instead of arguing over the point, proved the emperor right). Any wonder Abduh failed? Will a 21st century Abduh fare any better? [Pope Benedict XVI at Regensburg, September 12, 2006. Available online at Catholic World News, http://www.cwnews .com/news/viewstory .cfm?recnum=46474.]

[124] Donald Malcom Reid.

Laden's right-hand man, Ayman al-Zawahiri, is[125] a Muslim Brotherhood alumnus who personally studied at the feet of Sayyid Qutb, the Brotherhood's chief ideologue.[126]

The Muslim Brotherhood

Given its current geopolitical importance, and threat represented by the numerous terrorist groups it spawned, it is worth taking a few moments to learn a bit about the Muslim Brotherhood. The Muslim Brotherhood (*Al Ikwhan Al Muslimun* in Arabic) was founded in 1928 by an Egyptian school teacher, Gassan al-Banna "in reaction to the 1924 abolition of the caliphate by Turkish reformer Kemal Ataturk."[127] Though originally conceived as an instrument of "spiritual and moral reform," it soon expanded into the political arena. By the end of World War II, the Brotherhood could claim 500,000 members in Egypt, with additional branches throughout the Middle East.[128]

The 1952 revolution that ended Britain's occupation of Egypt and brought Gamal Abdul Nasser to power brought with it Nasser's ideology of Arab nationalism—essentially a secular version of the Brotherhood's dream of uniting all of the former Ottoman lands into a single Arab state. Though they differed in one crucial respect—Nasser sought a modern, essentially secular Arab state, while the

---

125 Or should that be, "was"? At the time of this writing (August 2008), there are news reports that Zawahiri was critically wounded in a U.S. attack on terrorist hideouts in Pakistan. By the time you are reading this, if we are fortunate, Zawahiri may be dead.

126 Marc Erikson, "Islamism, fascism and terrorism (Part 2), *Asia Times*, November 8, 2002.

127 Marc Erikson, "Islamism, fascism and terrorism (Part 1), *Asia Times*, November 5, 2002. The date of the Muslim Brotherhood's founding and the reason for its founding are significant. Obviously, a movement that began at least a generation before Israel's restoration and the deliverance of its Jewish citizens from foreign occupation, and several generations before the post-Yom Kippur War creation of the "Palestinian people" and the call for a "Palestinian state" can have only a *post hoc* relation to either. In fact, all jihadist organizations, including the Muslim Palestinian ones, are branches of the same tree and their fight is with *all* infidels, not just Israel. The movement's core mission demonstrably is not the liberation of "oppressed peoples" (as its failure to condemn the oppression of their co-religionists by Hamas in Gaza or of Christians, by the Muslim majorities in Gaza, Judea and Samaria proves). The movement's goal is not liberation, but subjugation—of non-Muslims in fulfillment of Mohammed's deathbed command, "Let there not be two religions in Arabia." (Bernard Lewis, *The Crisis of Islam: Holy War and Holy Terror* (New York: Random House Trade Paperbacks, 2004), xxix) and then extension of Mohammed's command to the rest of the world. The "Palestinian question" matters only insofar as it returns additional land to Muslim rule.

128 Marc Erikson, November 5, 2002.

Brotherhood's goal was to reconstitute the defunct, Islamic, caliphate—the two had enough in common to work together, at least for a while, with unfortunate consequences for the Copts. Nasser's alliance with the Brotherhood required him to at least partially embrace its Islamist goals and so, the pendulum that had been swinging toward greater tolerance of Egypt's non-Muslims began, once again, to swing back. Where before Nasser, Copts made up a large part of the civil servant class, holding such positions as governor, minister of foreign affairs and even prime minister, Copts now found themselves, once again, on the outs, "excluded from the top echelons of political and administrative bodies."[129]

Still, at the end of the day, Nasser was an Arab nationalist, not an Islamic fundamentalist, who instituted this new anti-Christian policy not from conviction, but solely as a sop to the Muslim Brotherhood who "played a large role" in Nasser's rise to power. As the Brotherhood's demands increased and became more extreme, the initially cordial relations between Nasser and the Brotherhood were bound to fray. The final straw came when the Brotherhood, inspired by the radical ideas of Sayyid Qutb, demanded that Nasser put Egypt under full Shari'a law. Nasser balked and the Brotherhood tried to assassinate him.[130] In the purge that followed, six Brothers were executed and 4,000 arrested. Thousands more fled the country. When, in 1965, a second attempt on Nasser's life failed, Qutb himself was imprisoned, tortured and, the following year, hanged.[131]

Qutb died in 1966, but the organization he helped found lived on and flourishes to this day, despite repeated attempts to outlaw it. In 1980, Qutb's dream of Islamizing

129 Saad Eddin Ibrahim.
130 Marc Erikson, "Islamism, fascism and terrorism (Part 3), Asia Times, December 12, 2002.
131 Ibid.

Egypt, thwarted by Nasser, was greatly advanced by Nasser's successor, Anwar Sadat, who amended the Egyptian constitution to make Islam "the Religion of the State" and Shari'a "the principal source of legislation."[132] In 2005, the Brotherhood held demonstrations in a dozen cities and towns[133] and early in 2007, the administration of current President Hosni Mubarak was rocked when the Brotherhood unexpectedly won 20 percent of the seats in the Egyptian legislature.

The Copts Today

Here, I must point out that, in the international community's failure even to note, let alone protest, Sadat's elevation of Shari'a, we have a textbook example of the international community's abject willingness, to be discussed in more detail later, to ignore the persecution of Christians in order to appease Muslims. At the same time the international community was feting Anwar Sadat for making peace with the Jewish state, Sadat was enshrining Islamic Shari'a law into Egypt's constitution, to the great detriment of her Christians. As Walid Phares, professor of Middle East studies and ethnic conflict at Florida University, describes:

> In the wake of the Camp David agreements, . . . a wave of governmental repression shook the Coptic community. Pope Shenouda[134] was imprisoned, Coptic quarters in Cairo were under siege, and numbers of Christians were either jailed by the authorities or killed by Islamists.[135]

---

[132] *Egyptian Constitution, Article* 2, available online at http://www.egypt.gov.eg /English/laws/Constitution/chp_one/part_one.asp. Not that these concessions to Islamic fundamentalism garnered many Brownie points for Sadat. The next year, he was assassinated—by Muslim fundamentalists, as retribution for signing a peace agreement with Israel.
[133] Daniel Williams, "Banned Group Leads Dissent in Egypt," *The Washington Post*, May 23, 2005.
[134] Patriarch of Coptic Christendom, essentially the Coptic equivalent of the Catholic Pope.
[135] Walid Phares, "Middle East Christians: The Captive Nations," p. 27.

The world plainly sees that the concessions Israel made at Oslo gained her precisely nothing. But how many of us know how the Oslo Accords affected Egypt's Christians?

> After the signing of the Oslo I and II agreements, Islamist attacks on Copts increased at an alarming rate. *In the region, the "peace process" was totally negative as far as the Christians were concerned.*[136]

And so it remains to this day. For example, the Egyptian government continues to enforce the Ottoman-era Hamayonic Decree that harshly restricts the building, repairing and remodeling of non-Muslim places of worship. For Christians, this means:

- Presidential permission is needed to build, repair or remodel a church;
- No church can be built within 100 meters of a mosque;
- If a new church is to be situated near a utility, the church must get the utility's permission;
- The church cannot be built if the local Muslims object.[137]

Predictably, with such restrictions, getting all the required permits, from all the required parties, can, and does, take years. And, of course, at the end of the years of red tape and waiting, permission to build ultimately may be denied. Indeed, *the very act of complying with the requirements* may lead to denial. Note the second point above, the prohibition against building a church within 100 meters of a mosque. What if, during the years the church is awaiting its permits, construction begins on a mosque (which never has to wait so

---

[136] Ibid," p. 27. (emphasis added)
[137] "Africa: Egypt," *U.S. State Department Religious Freedom Reports 2006*, available online. Go to http://www .persecution.org/suffering/country_info.php and click on link to "Egypt."

long for *its* permits) within 100 meters of the proposed church site. Then, obviously, the church cannot be built on the originally proposed site.[138] It is not at all unheard of for authorities, deliberately, to make whatever circumstantial changes are necessary to stop a church from being built, such as by slowing a church's application process while simultaneously fast-tracking a mosque's application to build within 100 meters of the proposed church site.

As recently as 2005, a church needed the President's personal permission to do so much as fix a toilet or replace a broken window. The law has since been changed to decision-making farther down the bureaucratic food chain, but far from making the process easier for Christians', the new law actually can make it worse because "lower officials are more easily influenced by extremist elements."[139] And a congregation awaiting its new-church permit had better not even think about conducting a Christian service in a private home. A new law, enacted in 2007, forbids Christians to hold a "religious meeting" in "unapproved" places and at "unapproved" times. For one Christian tourist, this meant that Christians literally could not even "gather in a room to pray together."[140]

In fairness to Egyptian president Mubarak, while a presidential decree still is required to build a new church, "President Mubarak reportedly has approved all requests for permits presented to him," including a $2.09 million cathedral able to accommodate 6,000 worshipers, and the rate of issuing permits has accelerated.[141] But in other cases, the multi-year delays continue, new restrictions have been added and where restrictions have been relaxed, local

---

[138] Ibid.
[139] Ibid.
[140] Joe Walker, *felix hominum*, April 29, 2007 http://joewalker.blogs.com /felixhominum/2007/04/out_of_egypt_ha.html
[141] For example, the issuance rate has increased from 12 Presidential decrees in the period June 30, 2004 to July 1, 2005, to 65 in the following 12-months. "Egypt—International Religious Freedom Report 2006."

authorities often circumvent them by, for example, "refus[ing] to process applications without certain 'supporting documents' that were virtually impossible to obtain [such as] a presidential decree authorizing the existence of a church which had been established during [Egypt's] monarchical era."[142] Nor does Mubarak's willingness to grant permission (and who is to say that future presidents will be equally willing?) change the fact that churches are required to get such permission in the first place while mosques are not.

Of course, the president cannot grant permission until he actually receives the request. And even after they get permission, Christians who want to build a new church in Egypt face bureaucratic obstacles that mosques do not:

> Interior Ministry delays—in some instances indefinitely—cause many requests to reach the President slowly or not at all. Some churches have complained that local security officials have blocked church repairs or improvements even when a permit has been issued. Others suggest unequal enforcement of the regulations pertaining to church and mosque projects.[143]

How bad is it? One new church waited 18 *years* for its construction permit, only to see the site vandalized shortly after the start of construction. Another, existing, church has been waiting *fifty* years (as of September 2006) for a *re*construction permit. These are not uncommon examples: a 2006 State Department report on religious freedom cites numerous additional instances of local authorities delaying,

---

[142] "Egypt—International Religious Freedom Report 2006, *Bureau of Democracy, Human Rights, and Labor, U.S. Department of State*. Available online at http://www.state.gov/g/drl/rls/irf/2006/71420.htm.
[143] Ibid.

denying or halting construction, as well as acts of vandalism by the local population.[144]

The same report also describes physical attacks on churches, and on the Christians who pray in them. On October 19, 2005, a Muslim man, enraged about a play that "purportedly blasphemed Islam," "assaulted a novitiate and a lay worker" at Alexandria's Mar Guirguis (St. George) Church. A few days later, a riot at the same church, by a mob estimated at 1,000[145] to 5,000, killed three, wounded dozens and ultimately had to be put down with sticks, tear gas[146] and rubber bullets.[147] Ironically, the play that sparked the violence was about "the dangers of extremism."[148]

Note that the riot occurred after Friday (the Muslim Sabbath) prayers in a nearby mosque.[149] May 11, 2007, the day a mob of over 500 Muslims burned 27 Christian homes and shops, injuring at least 10 Copts, also fell on a Friday and that riot, too, began after Friday prayers—in this case, when an imam incited worshippers to "rise and defend Islam against 'Christian infidels'," who were rumored to be planning to convert the private house in which they had been worshipping into a church. This is a recurring pattern, and not just in Egypt. An imam rails against some real or imagined slight to Islam during Friday prayers and worshippers pour into the streets, to vent their rage on the local Christians.[150]

Again in fairness to Mubarak, I note that, as these examples show, violence against Christian Egyptians is being fomented by *ad hoc* mobs at the local level; it is not a

---

[144] Ibid.
[145] Ibid.
[146] "Three killed in Egypt church riot," *BBC News*, http://news.bbc.co.uk/2/hi/middle_east/4366232.stm.
[147] "Egypt—International Religious Freedom Report 2006."
[148] "Three killed in Egypt church riot."
[149] "Egypt—International Religious Freedom Report 2006."
[150] "Coptic Christians Call for End of Religious Persecution, *Catholic Information Service for Africa (allAfrica.com)*, May 25, 2007, http://allafrica.com/stories/200705250716.html.

policy of the Egyptian government, notwithstanding the occasional participation of police and other local government officers, who certainly are freelancing. To my knowledge, no one accuses Hosni Mubarak or his of abetting, let alone ordering, violence against Christians. Indeed, Mubarak has been credited with making sincere efforts to discourage it.[151] While admittedly, this provides small comfort to a Copt suffering at the hands of a crowd of angry Muslims, where physical attacks on Egyptian Christians is concerned, Mubarak's sins seem to be more of omission than of commission— his failure or inability to take effective action against perpetrators, including people in his own government, of anti-Christian violence, or to foster an atmosphere in which Christian persecution would be less likely.

Your Papers, Please

As is typical in authoritarian countries, every Egyptian must carry an identity card. Egyptian identity cards, however, in addition to the usual information, also include the bearer's religion. This matters because an Egyptian cannot apply for a job without one and the bearer's faith, there on the card for all to see, does bear on where, and how far, he can go in Egyptian society. Imagine that you had to carry such a card or that your drivers license or Social Security card listed your religion. Imagine that you could not, by law, start a business, register your child for school or even open a bank account without declaring your religion. Imagine being stopped by a police officer conducting a "random check," who demands that you produce your identity card and if you cannot, being "detained" until

---

[151] "Egypt—International Religious Freedom Report 2006.

someone provides one.[152] In Egypt, Christians do not have to imagine; it is the law.

Christians Under Shari'a

Marriage, divorce, alimony, child custody and burial, all are governed by religious law—Shari'a for Muslims, canon law for Christians and Jewish law for Jews—but only if *none* of the parties is a Muslim, in which case Shari'a governs for *both* parties, regardless of faith. In the case of a Muslim man married to a Christian woman, Shari'a governs both spouses *and all children, including adults.*[153] Conversely, if the man is a Christian and the woman Muslim . . . well, actually, there is no such thing: A Muslim woman cannot marry a non-Muslim man, period. A non-Muslim man who wishes to marry a Muslim woman must convert to Islam.[154] If the couple try to circumvent Shari'a by marrying outside the country, their marriage will not be recognized in Egypt.[155] And if the man is Muslim when they marry, but later converts to another faith, *his wife must divorce him.* Converts from Islam also lose custody of their children.[156] And speaking of children, if one spouse is Muslim, the children are Muslim. If a non-Muslim converts to Islam, any children, *including adult children,* automatically become Muslim, too,[157] and when young children start school, "Children with Muslim names are enrolled in Islamic classes, regardless of their parents' wishes."[158]

A female Muslim heir, by law, is entitled to only half the amount of a male heir's inheritance, and even that only if she

---

[152] Ibid. By the way, it is even worse for Baha'is, who cannot even *get* an identity card, which permits only the listing of one of the three "heavenly faiths"—Muslim, Christian or Jew. Law 263 "bans Baha'i institutions and community activities, and a 1961 presidential decree stripped Baha'is of legal recognition."
[153] "Egypt—International Religious Freedom Report 2006.
[154] To be fair, the Coptic Orthodox church, too, forbids a Coptic man to marry a Christian woman and excommunicates a Christian woman who marries a Muslim man, but this is strictly religious, not civil law, as is Shari'a.
[155] "Egypt—International Religious Freedom Report 2006.
[156] *Egypt,* Christian Solidarity Worldwide.
[157] "Egypt—International Religious Freedom Report 2006.
[158] "Africa: Egypt," *U.S. State Department Religious Freedom Reports 2006.*

is a Muslim; a *Christian* widow of a Muslim man has no legal right to inherit anything beyond what is stipulated in the deceased's will.[159]

In February 2006, a Christian medical resident was denied employment by the Minya University pediatrics department because of her faith. (The Muslim department chairman, to his credit, resigned.)[160] Similarly, according to the most recent information this writer could find (2002), there are no Christian university heads or deans.[161]

Only Muslims are allowed to teach the Arabic language in Egyptian schools[162], often from the Koran, even to Christian students. The Coptic language, on the other hand, is not taught at all, nor are the first six centuries, A.D., of Egyptian history, when Christians were the majority in Egypt.[163]

Cairo's prestigious Al-Azhar University is publicly funded, meaning that Copts' taxes help support it, but Copts are not permitted to study there. Every school has a mosque; none has a church.[164] And speaking of mosques, Coptic taxes support those, too, and pay the imams' salaries. Churches and priests, on the other hand, receive no public funding.[165]

"Insulting Islam"

Spurred by the rise of Islamic fundamentalism, "[t]he distinction between civil law and Shari'a ... has been deliberately eroded,"[166] to the point where, as in other Muslim countries, "insulting Islam" is a crime for which people have gone to prison. In August 2000, a Copt named Sourial Isshak was sentenced to three years with hard labor

---

[159] "Egypt—International Religious Freedom Report 2006.
[160] Ibid.
[161] *Egypt,* Christian Solidarity Worldwide.
[162] Adelman and Kuperman.
[163] *Egypt,* Christian Solidarity Worldwide.
[164] Ibid.
[165] "Egypt—International Religious Freedom Report 2006.
[166] *Egypt,* Christian Solidarity Worldwide.

when several Muslims testified that they heard Isshak "curse Islam."[167]

Anti-Christian Violence

By coincidence, Isshak committed his "crime" just one day before the notorious "El-Kosheh II" incident. El-Kosheh is a village in Upper Egypt. On Friday, December 31, 1999 (another example of Muslim violence starting on a Friday), a dispute between a Muslim woman and a Christian shopkeeper[168] erupted into a "three-day rampage"[169] that quickly spread to neighboring villages. Before it was over, one Muslim and 21 Copts lay dead amid the destruction of 260 Coptic homes and businesses."[170] Police, who had arrived on the scene 48 hours earlier[171], "stood by passively or, even worse, actively participated in the attacks."[172] Though all but one of the dead were Christian[173] and no Christians were accused of killing the sole Muslim victim, who in any event was killed not in El-Kosheh, but in a neighboring village[174], Egyptian authorities blamed Muslim *and Christian* "delinquent elements" for the incident.

Of 96 Muslims tried for El-Kosheh, 92 were acquitted. Of the four who were not, one was sentenced to 10 years imprisonment for possession of an illegal weapon; the other three were given one-year sentences for burning a truck trailer. No one was convicted of any of the murders.[175] Outrage over the verdicts led to a retrial in 2003 and this time one of the defendants, the one convicted of possessing

---

[167] "Egypt Jails Christian for Three Years for "Insulting Islam," *Christianity Today*, August 1, 2000. Available online at http://ctlibrary.com/15853.
[168] "Kosheh file reopened," *Al-Ahram Weekly* (Egypt), March 20-26, 2003. Available online at http://weekly.ahram .org.eg/print/2003/630/eg10.htm.
[169] "EGYPT: Shock Acquittals at El Kosheh Retrial," *Christian Solidarity Worldwide*, February 28, 2003. Available online at http://jmm.aaa.net.au/articles/10721. htm.
[170] "Egypt Jails Christian for Three Years for "Insulting Islam," *Christianity Today*, August 1, 2000. Available online at http://ctlibrary.com/15853.
[171] "El Kosheh," *Association for Human Rights Legal Aid*, undated. Available online at http://www.ahrla.org/en/enrep/list/rpkoshh.html.
[172] "EGYPT: Shock Acquittals at El Kosheh Retrial."
[173] *Egypt*, Christian Solidarity Worldwide.
[174] "EGYPT: Shock Acquittals at El Kosheh Retrial."
[175] *Egypt*, Christian Solidarity Worldwide.

an illegal weapon in the first trial, was found guilty of murder—of the lone *Muslim* victim. As at the first trial, no one was convicted of murdering a Christian. This time, even the government prosecutor was outraged and formally contested the verdict. "There is no doubt that 21 people were killed," said Prosecutor General Maher Abdel Wahid, "and the killers must be brought to justice."[176] The Coptic Bishop Wissa, whose diocese includes El-Kosheh, merely stated the obvious when he said, "If the perpetrators of the murders are allowed to walk free, it will be seen as a green light to kill Christians."[177]

One final point about El-Kosheh II: Obviously, it would not be called El-Kosheh *II* had there not first been an "El-Kosheh *I*." On August 14, 1998, the bodies of two murdered Christians were found in El-Kosheh. Even though locals identified three Muslim men as the perpetrators,[178] Egyptian police detained 1,000 *Christians*. Many were tortured, including Shaiboub William Arsal, who was "hung upside down by his feet, beaten, tied to a chair and given electric shocks to sensitive parts of his body."[179] Arsal was subsequently tried, convicted of murder and sentenced to fifteen years with hard labor, where, as of 2007, he remains, awaiting appeal, even after two army officers admitted that their testimony, key in convicting Arsal, was false and given under duress.[180]

Unfortunately, El-Koshehs I and II are far from isolated examples of Muslim Egyptian anti-Christian violence.[181]

---

[176] Interview in Al-Ahaly (Egypt), undated. Cited in "EGYPT: Shock Acquittals at El Kosheh Retrial."
[177] "EGYPT: Shock Acquittals at El Kosheh Retrial."
[178] "Campaign for Shaiboub William Arsal, *Christian Solidarity Worldwide*, April 12, 2004. Available online at http://www.csw.org.uk/LtstCampaigns/if/Egypt/ShaiboubWilliamArsal_if.htm.
[179] *Egypt*, Christian Solidarity Worldwide.
[180] "Campaign for Shaiboub William Arsal."
[181] Numerous additional, more recent examples can be found in the category, "Egypt," on my Web site, , http://www.thechristianstate.com.

Beyond El-Kosheh

On January 17, 2006, in the village of Edyssat, a rumor that Copts were about to repair—not build, just repair—a church, sent Muslims into the streets, where they set fire to the church and attacked local Christian homes, putting nine Copts in the hospital, one of whom later died from his injuries.[182]

On February 20, 2006, violence erupted in the village of Azba Wasef, when local Muslims, hearing a rumor that a banquet hall being built by Christians was really a church, tried to burn it down. The hall survived, but the mob did manage to "set fire to at least four Christian homes," injuring 11.[183]

On April 14, 2006, "A man" stabbed 17 Christians at three churches in Alexandria, wounding 16 and killing one. Authorities claimed that the man was mentally ill and acting alone, but one Christian wondered: "How could one man go to so many churches at once? Is he Superman?" During the victim's funeral procession, the Christian mourners' chant of "With our blood, with our soul, we will sacrifice for you, Christ," angered nearby Muslims, prompting them to chant back the Muslim slogan, "There is no God but God." It "was the Christian funeral procession," a Muslim taxi driver said in explanation for the *two days* of violence that ensued. "They insulted Muslims." Apparently, in Egypt, merely proclaiming one's faith, if that faith is not Islam, "insults Muslims." But not, to their credit, all Muslims: the next day, a procession of Muslim and Christian clergy marched together peacefully, chanting, "Long live the crescent and the cross."[184]

---

[182] Nina Shea, Director, Center for Religious Freedom, Freedom House, *Testimony Before Committee on International Relations, U.S. House of Representatives, Subcommittee on Africa, Global Human Rights and International Operations*, March 16, 2006.
[183] Ibid.
[184] Ursula Lindsey, "Egyptian riots reveal wide religious divide," *Christian Science Monitor*, April 19, 2006.

On February 9, 2007, Muslims torched four Christian shops in the town of Armant.[185]

On February 13, 2007, "unknown assailants" threw "burning, kerosene-soaked cotton" into two Christian homes, ostensibly on—yes—another rumor, this time of a romance between a Christian man and a Muslim woman. However, according to a Cairo weekly, the real cause was a different rumor—that a Christian photographer was taking nude photos of Muslim women and blackmailing them into converting to Christianity. Fortunately, the fires were quickly extinguished, but when six family members reported the assault to the police, the police did not even bother to look for a Muslim perpetrator, opting instead to detain the *Christian* victims for 36 hours, releasing them only after they signed statements that they, the Christians, set fire to their own homes.[186]

On March 9, 2007, Muslims ambushed and killed Christian Attia and his son, Magdy. Again, rather than seek out the Muslim perps, the police charged Attia's *other son*, Essmat, with "carrying a weapon, even though no weapon was found."[187]

On May 11, 2007, on a rumor that Christians were secretly building a church, the imam of a mosque in the village of Bemha incited worshippers to "defend Islam," which they then proceeded to do by "attack[ing] 70 houses, looting shops and wounding many Christians."[188] May 11, 2007 fell on a Friday, so here is yet another example of a "anti-Christian threefer": another Friday, another rumor and

---

[185] Article in *Sawt al-Umma* (Cairo), February 19, 2007. Cited in "Egypt: Copts Detained After Anti-Christian Attack," *Compass Direct News*, February 22, 2007. Available online at http://compassdirect.org/en/display.php?page=news&lang=en&length=long&idelement=4780&backpage=summaries.
[186] Ibid.
[187] R. Iscandar, "American Coptic Union Calls for U.S. Sanctions Against Egypt," *Christian Newswire*, March 20, 2007. Available online at http://www .christiannewswire.com/news/367392535.html.
[188] "Egyptian Coptic Christians Attacked By Violent Mobs," *Journal Chretien*, June 25, 2007. Originally reported in Coptic newspaper *Watani* Compass Direct.

another call to violence by the imam at the conclusion of services.

On June 7, 2007, an argument broke out in the Christian enclave of Zwyet Abdel-Qader "between a Christian truck driver and a Muslim teenager who refused to move out of the way to let the truck pass." The next day, Muslims looted and vandalized Christian shops in a riot that took police 90 minutes to quell.[189]

On June 12, 2007, an argument between two construction workers — one Muslim, one Christian — led to rioting during which bottles and stones were thrown at the Holy Virgin's Church in Dekheila.[190]

On September 24, 2007, "sectarian clashes" erupted in Alexandria on rumors (yes, another rumor) of a "love story" between a young Christian man and a Muslim woman. Or was there, perhaps, another reason? According to one of the Christian man's relatives, "The Muslim guys are only jealous because our family has a car and two cafeterias while being Christian." In any case, as a Christian witness to the "sectarian clashes" described it, "Throngs of people were attacking each other. A man wearing a face veil was throwing stones at Christians, and women were standing in balconies cheering on the Muslims, shouting 'God is Great' [and] 'Christians are sons of dogs.'"

On October 26, 2007, in yet another instance of Muslim violence beginning "after Friday prayers," Muslims "clash[ed]" with Christians "after Friday prayers" to protest the extension of a monastery. 20 people were injured in the violence, which Police required reinforcements to quell.[191]

---

[189] Ibid.
[190] Ibid.
[191] Salah Nasrawi, "Muslim, Christians clash in Egypt," *AP*, October 26, 2007.

On December 12, 2007, Muslims "surround[ed] and smash[ed] up" a Christian store "where they suspected a Muslim girl was having sex with two Christian boys."

On December 16, 2007, the day after a Christian shop-owner accused a Muslim woman of shoplifting, Muslim rioters vandalized 13 Christian-owned shops and a church.[192]

A Rising Tide Lifts All Islamic Fundamentalists

This increase in Muslim-on-Christian violence comes amid a rising tide of Islamic fundamentalism. For example,

> Observers believe that Alexandria is gradually embracing religious radicalism and a form of bigotry alien to its reputation as a tolerant metropolis. Despite being a summer resort, popular for its long stretches of beaches and sea activities, the attire of women in particular is becoming more and more conservative even on hot summer days. Men wearing ankle-length robes and women dressed in black from head to toe except for two slits for the eyes are a common sight.

Others agree that "'the overly-conservative religious groups had a role in changing Alexandria.' An Alexandrian recounted how a sheikh kept intimidating him after discovering that he was a Christian. 'He would ask me why I believed in the Bible. I used to run from him.'"[193]

Cyber-Shari'a

In Egypt, as around the world, the Internet has sparked an "infolution" by enabling ordinary citizens to disseminate their messages to millions. Egyptian bloggers are entering

---

[192] Ibid.
[193] Pakinam Amer, "Rumours of love affair spark sectarian clashes in Egypt," Deutsche Presse-Agentur, September 24, 2007.

cyberspace to alert the international community to the plight of Egypt's threatened Copts—and the Egyptian government is acting aggressively to keep that message from getting out. When Hala Helmy Botros wrote about the treatment of Copts on her blog, *Aqbat Bela Hodood* (Copts Without Borders), authorities cut her phone line and her Internet connection and placed her under surveillance. Strangers beat her father, saying, "This is a present from your daughter." When her father reported the beating to the police, he was forced to sign a blank sheet of paper, "to which they added a statement in which he appeared to accuse his daughter of responsibility for the attack." When Hala tried to fly to a conference in the United States, she was physically removed from the plane, told she could not leave the country, questioned for several hours and ordered to appear in court. A week later, police raided her home to arrest her. Failing to find Hala, they took her husband instead and forced him to sign a statement guaranteeing his wife's appearance three days later. Appearing in court on the appointed day with two lawyers, Botros was "questioned about her Internet posts and accused of 'spreading false news' and of 'disrupting social harmony between the Muslim and Christian communities.'" She was released on bail, but questioned again the next day.

Though it took awhile, the intimidation ultimately had the desired effect: Fearing by now for her own and her family's safety, Botros not only shut down her blog, but stopped posting on other sites about the treatment of Christian Egyptians. And yet, still, "[s]he is being watched by plainclothes police, her telephone is tapped and her e-mail is being monitored."[194]

---

[194] "Months of harassment force Copt blogger to censor herself," *Reporters Without Borders*, August 14, 2006.

Hala Botros is a Christian, but there are Muslim bloggers, too, such as 22-year-old former law student Abdel Kareem Nabil Suleiman. Suleiman, a liberal Muslim who condemns the persecution of Egypt's Christians and dares to speak publicly against it has the distinction of being the first Egyptian blogger to be prosecuted (or should that be, persecuted?) for his blogging after he wrote an article accusing al-Azhar University—the one that does not admit Christians—of "promoting extreme ideas." Another article, "The Naked Truth of Islam as I Saw It," "accused Muslims of savagery" during the October 19, 2005 riot at the Mar Guirguis Church that I described earlier.[195] He also called some of Mohammed's companions "terrorists," and likened President Hosni Mubarak "to dictatorial pharaohs who ruled ancient Egypt."

On February 22, 2007, Suleiman was sentenced to three years imprisonment for "inciting hatred of Islam" and an additional year for "insulting" President Hosni Mubarak.[196] Harsh as this sentence is, the court actually was more merciful to Suleiman than his own family would have been: Shortly before the reading of the verdict, they disowned him and Suleiman's father demanded Shari'a law for his son, saying "Give him three days to repent; if he doesn't then kill him."[197]

Future Prospects

According to the United States Commission on International Religious Freedom's 2007 Report About Egypt:

> Serious problems of discrimination, intolerance, and other human rights violations against

---

[195] See page 51

[196] "UN secretary-general asked to raise imprisoned blogger's case with Egyptian president," *Reporters Without Borders*, March 27, 2007.

[197] Nabeel Abu Shal and Tamer Al-Sharqawy, "Kareem's Family Disowns Him; Father Wants Him Killed If He Does Not 'Repent,'" *Al-Masree Al-Yawm* (Egypt), February 18, 2007. "Kareem" in the article's title refers to Suleiman's blogging pseudonym, Abdul Kareem.

members of religious minorities ... remain widespread in Egypt. Over the past few years, the Egyptian government has adopted several measures to acknowledge the religious pluralism of Egypt's society, including increased efforts in promoting interfaith activity. *Yet the government has not taken sufficient steps to halt repression of and discrimination against religious believers, including the indigenous Coptic Orthodox Christians, or, in many cases, to punish those responsible for violence or other severe violations of religious freedom.*

Egypt remains on the Commission's Watch List, and the Commission continues to monitor the actions of the government of Egypt to see if the situation rises to a level that warrants designation as a "country of particular concern," or CPC. *Egypt has a poor overall human rights record that includes repressive practices which seriously violate freedom of thought, conscience, and religion or belief.*[198]

As for the future:

Human rights organizations inside the country are seriously concerned that Islamic extremism is advancing in Egypt, with detrimental effects on the prospects for democratic reform, religious tolerance, and the rights of women and girls and members of religious minorities.

Some believe that the government is not acting to its fullest ability to counteract this problem, especially in the areas of public

---

[198] "Egypt—International Religious Freedom Report 2006. (emphases added)

education and the media, where *extremist influence is growing.*[199]

I will give the last word on Egypt to two Egyptians — one Christian, one Muslim. First, Coptic Bishop Morcos Aziz Zakariya:

> The history of the Copts is full of constraints and discrimination. Quiet times are an exception. Currently, Copts are suffering outright discrimination, and we should not attempt to embellish this fact. *Matters are getting worse and the state is not moving one bit.*[200]

And second and finally, Egyptian, and Muslim, writer Mona Eltahawy, who in 2005 wrote, "Is Islam so fragile that Muslims need to riot to protect it?"[201]

Apparently, in Egypt, the answer is, yes.

Other Middle Eastern Countries

Egypt, Lebanon and the Palestinian territories have the largest, but by no means the only, Christian populations. So let's briefly examine some of the others.

Iran

According to the State Department, "The [Iranian] Government severely restricts freedom of religion. . . . All laws and regulations must be consistent with the official interpretation of the Shari'a." Zoroastrians, Jews, and Christians may practice their faiths, but only "within the limits of the law." Members of all three of these faiths "have reported imprisonment, harassment, intimidation, and discrimination."

---

[199] Ibid. (emphases added)
[200] Pakinam Amer, "Christian Copts: Between integration and dissent," *Kuwait Times*, July 9, 2007. (emphasis added)
[201] Mona Eltahawy, "Egypt's Christian-Muslim divide," *International Herald Tribune*, November 10, 2005.

Non-Muslims are forbidden by law to serve in any elected body, senior government or military position, with the exception of five specially-designated seats in Iran's legislative body, the *majlis*. Of these five seats, three are reserved for Christians.

Non-Muslims cannot be judges, security officers or public school principals. "Applicants for public sector employment [are] screened for their adherence to and knowledge of Islam." Officially, the army must be Islamic though, in practice, non-Muslims do serve. However, in keeping with the Koran's stricture that no non-Muslim may rule over a Muslim, "the law forbids non-Muslims from holding officer positions over Muslims." Non-Muslims with college degrees can be officers during mandatory military service, but cannot be career military officers.[202]

Iranian law requires non-Muslim grocery shop owners to declare their religion on their storefronts.[203]

Non-Muslims may not proselytize among Muslims. "The Government vigilantly [enforces] its prohibition on proselytizing activities by evangelical Christians by closely monitoring their activities, closing their churches, and arresting Christian converts. . . ." The government restricts evangelical services to Sundays and church officials must inform the Ministry of Information and Islamic Guidance before admitting new members to their congregations. The government also pressures Christians "to sign pledges that they would not evangelize Muslims or allow Muslims to attend church services."[204]

Churchgoers in Tehran, especially those of Tehran's Assembly of God congregation, have been harassed,

---

[202] "Iran—International Religious Freedom Report 2006, *Bureau of Democracy, Human Rights, and Labor, U.S. Department of State*. Available online at http://www.state.gov/g/drl/rls/irf/2006/71421.htm.
[203] Ibid.
[204] Ibid.

including stationing Revolutionary Guards outside to
discourage Muslims or converts from entering.

Iraq

Lost amid all the debate and reporting—and much
*mis*reporting—on Iraq is the plight of the country's
Christians. Has anyone speculated on what would happen
to *them* if the U.S. were prematurely to abandon Iraq?

On April 18, 2007, an "unknown armed Islamic group"
warned local Christians, "Get rid of the cross or we will burn
your churches." In one case, "Muslim extremists took the
situation into their own hands: they climbed onto the roof
[of the Church of St. George] and ripped out the cross,"
while issuing the Christians an ultimatum to, "convert to
Islam or die," and a *fatwa* "forbidding Christians to wear the
cross or make any religious gesture" and that "permits the
confiscation of goods and properties" of Christians forced to
flee their homes.[205]

On April 23, 2007, a suicide bombing in the northern
Christian village of Tell-el-skop killed 10 and injured 140,
prompting the Bishop of Kurdistan to "beg" the Pope to
intervene, saying, "the Church in Iraq is in great danger."[206]

On May 30, 2007, the "People's Foundation for the Master
al-Mahdi Army" issued a letter warning Christian women to
don the veil. If a woman refused, her husband or father was
required to "guide and educate her religiously in order to
convince her. If she is not convinced still, then they must
imprison her at home and do not expose her to the forbidden
interaction with men."[207]

---

[205] "Get rid of the cross or we will burn your churches," *Asia News*, April 18, 2007.
[206] "Bishop of Kurdistan: "the Church in Iraq is in great danger," *Asia News*, April 24, 2007.
[207] "The Mahdi army imposes the veil on Christian Women," *Asia News*, May 30, 2007. Available online at http://www.asianews.it/index.php?l=en&art=9409.

On June 3, 2007, gunmen assassinates a friar and three aides outside Mosul's Church of the Holy Spirit.[208]

On June 8, 2007, "an al Qaida-affiliated insurgent group" told Christians to "convert to Islam, marry your daughters to our fighters, pay an Islamic tax [the *jizyah*]—or leave with only the clothes on your back."[209]

On July 5, 2007, a group calling itself the Islamic Emirate of Mosul threatens to kidnap or kill all Christian students and employees of Mosul University and to behead "any Christian who will remain in the city."[210]

Christian Prospects: Changing for the Better?

On the other hand, it must be noted, all of the incidents I just described occurred before the initiation, and success, of the President Bush's "surge" strategy. Though today, even with the war won, one could not exactly accuse the Christians of living in a paradise on earth, we do see early signs that their condition may be changing for the better—a trend that, in fact, was nascent even before the appointment of General David Petraeus, the general responsible for implementing the new strategy. Michael Yon, an independent journalist who has self-embedded himself with the U.S. forces in Iraq, has for the past two years been reporting, and photographing, events on the ground. In his November 16, 2007 report, posted on his personal blog, Yon described a milestone event: the reopening of St. John's church in Baghdad and the welcoming back—by *Muslims*—of Iraqi Bishop Slemon Warduni. The report leads with a moving photo of Christians and Muslims, together, returning the cross to the dome atop the church in

---

[208] "A Chaldean priest and three deacons killed in Mosul," *Asia News*, June 3, 2007. Available online at http://www.asianews.it/index.php?l=en&art=9442.
[209] Leila Fadel and Hannah Allam, "Baghdad Christians threatened with tax, eviction," *Sacramento Bee*, June 8, 2007.
[210] "Islamic Group Driving Christians Away From Mosul," *Assyrian International News Agency*, July 5, 2007.

preparation for Bishop Warduni's arrival. According to Yon, as related to him by a U.S. soldier, LTC Stephen Michael,

> when al Qaeda came to Dora, they began harassing Christians first, charging them "rent." *It was the local Muslims, according to LTC Michael, who first came to him for help to protect the Christians in this area.* That's right. LTC Michael told me more than once that *the Muslims reached out to him to protect the Christians from al Qaeda.*[211]

Another photo shows the church's interior, its front pews filled with local Muslims, and below that photo, this caption:

> Today, Muslims mostly filled the front pews of St. John's. *Muslims who want their Christian friends and neighbors to come home.* The Muslims in this neighborhood worry that other people will take the homes of their Christian neighbors, and that the Christians ill never come back. And so they came to St. John's today in force, and they showed their faces, and they said, *"Come back to Iraq. Come home."* They wanted the cameras to catch it. They wanted to spread the word: *Come home.* Muslims keep telling me to get it on the news. *"Tell the Christians to come home to their country Iraq."*[212]

At the same time, busloads of Iraqis who sought refuge in surrounding states are returning to Iraq every day. One hopes that Christians are among them, that scenes like the one Michael Yon describes will be repeated, many times. Indeed, the Associated Press reported one church in eastern Baghdad being almost full for the 2007 Christmas mass and here, too, "Muslim clerics—both Sunni and Shiite—also attended the service in a sign of unity."

---

[211] Michael Yon, "Come Home," *Michael Yon: Online Magazine,* November 16, 2007, http://www.michaelyon-online.com/wp/come-home.htm.
[212] Ibid. (first emphasis added; remaining emphases in original)

I began this section by citing a news report of Muslims removing the cross from a church roof;. Later I cited Michael Yon's report of Muslims and Christians, together, putting a cross *on* a church. To this writer, that says it all.

But wait, as the TV pitchmen say, there's more. At the time of this writing, the Iraqi government and it's president, Nouri al-Maliki, have finally stepped up to the plate and pledged to protect Iraq's Christians.[213]   Given his, and our, successful routs of the Mahdi army and Al Qaeda, there is every reason to believe that Maliki will make good on his commitment.

And finally, Christian Iraqis are starting to take upon themselves the task of defending their community with the formation of the first Christian militias.[214]

How far the rehabilitation Iraq's Christian community will go, how much their lot will improve, I cannot say, but the situation improves day-by-day and certainly, by the time you are reading this, will have advanced beyond the facts I report here.

Syria

That Syria has been one of the countries in which Iraqi Christians have sought sanctuary, and that Syria has been accepting them,[215] points to Syria as one of the more, if not the most, Christian-tolerant of the Middle Eastern Muslim states. Make no mistake, Syria is a police state, but a secular one — by Muslim Middle Eastern standards, anyway — with a strictly enforced separation between "religion and police state" — a dictatorship under which all Syrians suffer equally, regardless of faith. For example, unlike Egypt, which, as we saw, publicly funds mosques, but not churches," all

---

213 "Maliki offers Iraqi Christians protection," *UPI*, July 30, 2008.

214 "Iraq's Christians form new militias to combat Islamic extremists," *Daily Telegraph* (London), July 27, 2008.

215 Now if they — and all the other Muslim states in the area — would only do the same for their fellow Muslims, who have been languishing in refugee camps for half a century.

governmentally-recognized Muslim, Jewish, and Christian communities, receive free utilities and are exempt from real estate taxes and personal property taxes on official vehicles." According to the State Department, "The late Grand Mufti's son Salah Kuftaro and his Abu Nur Islamic Institute continued to engage in a wide variety of activities promoting Christian-Muslim understanding" — and though it has no practical bearing on Christians, it is still interesting to note that, in May 2006, the Grand Mufti invited an American rabbi to speak at a mosque to an audience of over three thousand Muslims.[216]

This is not to say that there is *no* religious discrimination in Syria: for example, the Syrian constitution permits only a Muslim to be president and the government views Jehovah's Witnesses as "a politically motivated Zionist organization." Nevertheless, the State Department reports only "occasional reports of minor tensions between religious groups" and attributes these to "economic rivalries rather than religious affiliation."[217] Indeed, if Syria has a "religious problem," it is not with Christians, but with Muslims — radical Muslims, riding the same wave of Islamic fundamentalism roiling the entire Middle East. In response to this threat, "[t]he Government selects moderate Muslims for religious leadership positions and is intolerant of and suppresses extremist views of Islam."

Nevertheless, in Syria, as throughout the Middle East, small, but ominous, signs of cracks in Syria's secularist façade are beginning to appear. For example, during the period covered by the State Department's 2006 report on religious freedom,

---

[216] "Syria — International Religious Freedom Report 2006, *Bureau of Democracy, Human Rights, and Labor, U.S. Department of State.* Available online at http://www.state.gov/g/drl/rls/irf/2006/71432.htm.
[217] Ibid.

the [Syrian] Government sometimes encouraged negative—even violent—expressions of Islamic religious sentiment, at least in part to curry favor with the Syrian Sunni majority. The clearest example of this occurred on February 4, 2006, when the Government allowed Muslim groups to demonstrate publicly against the publication of the [Danish Mohammed] cartoons, and later failed to control a mob of several thousand Muslim protesters that attacked and set fire to the building housing the Danish, Swedish, and Chilean embassies, and later set fire to the Norwegian Embassy.[218]

On the other hand, as serious as these incidents are, we must recognize that the demonstration was in protest of an event that occurred in a foreign country and all the attacks were on foreign embassies, albeit foreign embassies located in Syria. They were not attacks on the indigenous Christian minority. So Christian Syrians are safe—for now. The only events that could their threaten their status would be a profound increase of Iranian influence not just on, but within, Syria à la Hitler's corruption of Mussolini;[219] or the overthrow of the government and its replacement by an Iranian-style fundamentalist Islamic regime (something we Americans will want to take care to prevent, as we did in Iraq, should Assad, for whatever reason, fall).

Or, God forbid, both.

---

[218] Ibid.

[219] So closely is Mussolini linked to Hitler that people tend to forget that, when Hitler came to power, Mussolini and fascism already had ruled Italy for many years (and, incidentally, been praised by such prominent Americans as Will Rogers). During those "pre-Hitler" years, Mussolini displayed no anti-Semitism, Jews were not discriminated against and, indeed were allowed to serve in government.

Jordan

Christian Jordanians enjoy relative security under King Abdullah. "The Government does not interfere with public worship by the country's Christian minority." However:

> all minor children of male citizens who convert to Islam are considered to be Muslim. Adult children of a male Christian who has converted to Islam become ineligible to inherit from their father if they do not also convert to Islam. In cases in which a Muslim converts to Christianity the conversion is not recognized legally by the authorities, and the individual continues to be treated as a Muslim in matters of family and property law.
>
> The Government traditionally reserves [four percent of] positions in the upper levels of the military for Christians; however, all senior command positions have been held by Muslims.[220]

Nevertheless, as with Syria, Christian Iraqis consider Jordan sufficiently Christian-tolerant to seek sanctuary within her borders, 750,000 having entered since the fall of Saddam Hussein.[221]

On February 20, 2008, Jordanian security forces arrested eight Evangelicals for proselytizing when local residents accused them of "offering humanitarian assistance to poor Muslim families and distributing fliers promoting Christianity," and "'enticing' impoverished youngsters by paying them money and calling on them to marry foreign girls."[222]

---

[220] "Jordan—International Religious Freedom Report 2006, *Bureau of Democracy, Human Rights, and Labor, U.S. Department of State*. Available online at http://www.state.gov/g/drl/rls/irf/2006/71424.htm.
[221] Ibid. And again, as with Syria, one needs to ask why Jordan cannot admit 750,000 *Muslim* refugees.
[222] "Jordan Arrests Evangelists," *The Media Line*. Available online at http://www .themedialine.org/news/news_detail.asp?NewsID=20625.

Turkey

Turkey straddles both the geographic division between "Europe" and "Arabia," and the theological one between Turkey's "secular" and "Islamic" elements—a division dramatized recently in the recent national election. The results of that election raises, for the first time in modern Turkish history, the question of which faction, the secular or the fundamentalist, ultimately will prevail. The answer, when it comes, could matter greatly to Turkey's Christians.

Modern Turkey is the realization of the vision of Kemal Attaturk, the great—and greatly transformational—leader who, by his will and forceful leadership, literally recreated the former seat of the Islamic Ottoman Empire, as a modern, secular, state. Today, Attaturk's vision is safeguarded by Turkey's army, which maintains a steady vigil against any resurgence of Islamic fundamentalism and has never hesitated to intervene, overrule and even remove civilian administrations that deviated from Attaturk's secularist vision. As far as the government (but alas, not always the Muslim citizenry) is concerned, Christians—and Jews—may practice their faiths freely. Though the Government does discourage public proselytizing, it does so strictly to preserve Turkey's secular character, discouraging proselytizing by *all* faiths, including Islam. Restrictions on overly religious public displays, to take one example, apply as much to Islam as to any other faith.

Which is not to say that official governmental discrimination, however mild, does not exist. Turkey's Human Rights Consultation Board reported that non-Muslims "were effectively barred from careers in state institutions, such as the armed forces, the Ministry of Foreign Affairs, the National Police, and the National Intelligence Agency." On the other hand, it is to Turkey's credit that it was a Turkish human rights organization that reported the discrimination—and when the report's two authors were prosecuted for writing it, a Turkish court acquitted them when the court determined the report to be true.[223]

Nevertheless, in line with the trend occurring throughout the Middle East, and despite the Turkey's secularist policies and traditions, Islamic fundamentalism has been growing in recent years among the general population, increasingly threatening Turkey's secularist tradition. In the words of Turkey's previous president, expressed in a 2006 speech, the "fundamentalist threat has reached a dangerous level"[224] and indeed, in 2007, both the current prime minister, Recep Tayyip Erdogan, and president, Abdullah Gul, have called for ending the government's ban on the wearing of Islamic headscarves in the country's universities.[225] On February 9, the Turkish Parliament "voted overwhelmingly" to amend the Turkish Constitution to allow women to wear headscarves at universities.

Earlier, I quoted a Christian Palestinian woman[226] who complained of being pressured by fundamentalist Muslim Palestinians to wear a headscarf, and of Malaysia's requirements that *all* female university students and police officers, Muslim and non-Muslim alike, *must* wear headscarves.[227] Secular Turks fear not only that the same thing might happen in Turkey, but that it may be just the first step towards putting Turkey completely under Shari'a law. As one secularist put it:

> "[Lifting the headscarf ban] has been presented
> as a liberty to cover the head, but in practice, it is

---

[223] "Turkey—International Religious Freedom Report 2006, *Bureau of Democracy, Human Rights, and Labor, U.S. Department of State.* Available online at http://www.state.gov/g /drl/rls/irf/2006/71413.htm.
[224] Ibid.
[225] "Turkish PM urges end to scarf ban," *BBC*, September 19, 2007.
[226] See page 13.
[227] See page 82.

going to evolve into a ban on uncovered hair," said Hikmet Sami Turk, a former justice minister . . . . "This is a starting point, that's the importance."

Nesrin Baytok, one of the secular lawmakers who voted against ending the ban, said much the same thing: "The decision [to end the ban] will bring further pressure on women. It will ultimately bring us Hezbollah terror, Al Qaeda terror and fundamentalism."[228]

Concerned that the AKP's rise to power and the way it has governed since attaining it, foreshadows the beginning of the end of Turkey as a secular state, the country's chief prosecutor indicted the AKP before the constitutional court, accusing it of "trying to turn Turkey, a secular democracy, into an Islamic state." The case failed by a single vote; however, the court did cut the party's funding in half as "a strong political warning by the court to the governing party against steering the country away from constitutionally mandated secularism."[229]

And the chief prosecutor, Abdurrahman Yalcinkaya, may not go gently into that fundamentalist night, either. Having failed to ban the party, Yalcinkaya is weighing the possibility of asking the constitutional court to ban Prime Minister Erdogan, personally, from "practicing politics."[230] In the meantime, several Turkish academics resigned their posts in protest after Turkey's president, Abdullah Gul, "vetoed the elections of university chiefs who oppose lifting the headscarf ban."[231]

---

[228] Sabrina Tavernise.

[229] "Court decides against banning governing party in Turkey," Sebnem Arsu, *International Herald Tribune*, July 30, 2008 http://www.iht.com/articles/2008/07/30 /Europe/turkey.php.

[230] "Reports say a new legal case could come to ban Turkish PM Erdogan," *HotNews Turkey.com*, August 7, 2008, http://www.hurriyet.com.tr/english/domestic/9597513 .asp?scr=1.

[231] "Turkish academics resign from their posts to protest Gul's rector choices," *HotNews Turkey.com*, August 7, 2008, http://www.hurriyet.com.tr/english/domestic/9596005 .asp?gid=244&sz=83399.

Would it not be ironic were the realization of Attaturk's and the secularists' goal—the transformation of Turkey into a modern state and the economic boom it has engendered—to be the cause of the secularists' problem, as a rural, religiously observant underclass becomes increasingly urban, prosperous and begins to enter the ranks of the formerly overwhelmingly secular elite? And yet, there are signs that that may, in fact, be exactly what is happening. At the ballot box, the rise of the Islamic fundamentalist underclass has translated into overwhelming majorities for conservative Muslim politicians such as Erdogan and Gul:

> Many secular Turks are concerned that Mr. Erdogan's Justice and Development Party now has such significant power, controlling the Parliament and the posts of president and prime minister, that party officials will impose their own conservative lifestyle on Turkey.[232]

Even before the new, apparently more fundamentalist-friendly government came to power, secular-minded judges "have been pushed into retirement or demoted and replaced by AKP sympathizers." ("AKP" stands for "Justice and Development Party," Turkey's majority political party, to which the president and prime minister belong.) Insufficiently Islamic teachers have suffered similar fates. Enforcement of the traditional ban on the public practice of religion is waning, with "wives of leading AKP figures wearing the religious *kapali* headgear to advertise their desire for the creation of a 'pure Islamic society.'" Businessmen, many of whom have prospered in Turkey's economic boom from "government contracts and import-

---

[232] Sabrina Tavernise, "Turkey's Parliament Lifts Scarf Ban," *New York Times*, February 10, 2008.

export quotas," donate generously to the AKP and openly express "their attachment to Islam"[233]

Especially worrisome is a potential transformation in Turkey's military, the traditional bulwark against Islamic fundamentalism, where Islamist officers are beginning to replace secularists. As Amir Taheri writes:

> Since 1980, the Turkish army has staged a coup once every 10 years, either to curb the radical left or to stop the Islamist right from seizing control of the state. A new coup could trigger a bitter power struggle and push the more radical Islamists toward violent, even terrorist, methods.[234]

But will there come a day when Islamic fundamentalism will threaten Turkey's secular society and the military does not intervene because there is no longer a secularist officer to give the order?[235]   Turkey's supreme military council apparently remains determined that there will not, and reinforced the point in 2008 "by appointing staunchly anti-Islamist General Ilker Basbug as army chief of staff.[236]

Recent Incidents of Concern

In January 2006, five assailants beat a Protestant church leader, threatening to kill him unless he renounced Christianity.

In February 2006, a 16-year-old boy, angered by the Danish Mohammed cartoons and shouting "God is great," shot to death a Catholic priest. That same month, a group of Muslim men seeking to "clean Turkey of non-Muslims" beat and threatened to kill a Catholic friar.

---

[233] Amir Taheri.
[234] Ibid.
[235] Amir Taheri.
[236] "Turkey appoints anti-Islamist army chief," Robert Tait, *The Guardian* (London), August 5, 2008.

In March 2006, a knife-wielding man shouting "anti-Christian slogans" entered a church and threatened worshippers.[237]

And then there is the April 11, 2007 incident, reported by media worldwide, in which "five Turkish fanatics" tortured three employees of a Christian publishing house and then slit their throats. One victim was stabbed 150 times. "This should serve as a lesson to the enemies of our religion," said the note the killers left at the scene. "We did it for our country."[238]

What will be Turkey's fate? On which side of the divide between freedom for all faiths, and submission to a single faith, will Turkey finally land? Is the day coming when Turks will go to sleep in an enlightened secular democracy and awaken in a benighted "Islamic republic," and what will it mean for Turkey's Christians?

Turkey's future remains to be written, the endurance of ultimate impact of Attaturk's vision yet to be seen. But here, in the words of the pseudonymous essayist, Spengler, is what is clear:

> If political Islam prevails in Turkey, what will emerge is not the same country in different coloration but . . . an entirely different nation. . . . Like a hologram, Turkey offers two radically different images when viewed from different angles. Turkish Islam, the ordering of the Anatolian villages and the Istanbul slums, represents a nation radically different [from] the secularism of the army, the civil service, the universities and the Western-leaning elite of

---

237 This incident and the two previous reported in "Turkey—International Religious Freedom Report 2006."
238 Annette Grossbongardt, "Christian Converts Live in Fear in Intolerant Turkey," *Der Spiegel* (Germany), April 23, 2007.

Istanbul. *If the Islamic side of Turkey rises, the result will be unrecognizable.*[239]

Israel

Is it not ironic that the average Middle Eastern Muslim enjoys more freedom, and more prosperity, in Israel than in any Muslim Middle Eastern state? So to, Israel's Christians, but it would be unfair to criticize the treatment of Christians in the surrounding Muslim countries while failing to acknowledge that discrimination against Christian Israelis, however mild, however rare, does occur. But even then, it is fair, and important, to state that, when Christian Israelis are discriminated against, the tendency is to discriminate against them not as Christians, but as Arabs, whom Israelis tend to "lump in" with their Muslim Arab counterparts. In addition — and ironic in a Jewish state — secular and non-orthodox Jews experience certain forms of discrimination that non-Jews, including Christians, do not, due to laws demanded by Israel's Orthodox Jewish community, a key constituency in Israeli politics. For example, Israel recently passed a law that will, for the first time, allow civil marriage, but only for non-Jews.[240] For Jews, Israel will continue to recognize only Orthodox Jewish marriage ceremonies. Non-Orthodox Jews wishing to marry in a different type of ceremony, or to marry a person of another faith, will need to do so outside the country.[241]

The Israeli government allocates money for religious institutions and has been accused of allocating such funds unequally. On the other hand, when non-Jewish groups challenge such allocations in Israeli courts, courts have ruled in favor of the non-Jewish plaintiffs. The U.S. State

---

[239] "Turkey in the throes of Islamic revolution?", Spengler, *Asia Times*, July 22, 2008, http://www.atimes.com/atimes/Middle_East/JG22Ak02.html. (emphasis added)
[240] Matthew Wagner, "Civil marriage to be option for non-Jews," *Jerusalem Post*, July 18, 2007.
[241] "Israel — International Religious Freedom Report 2006, *Bureau of Democracy, Human Rights, and Labor*, *U.S. Department of State*. Available online at http://www.state.gov/g/drl/rls/irf/2006/71423.htm.

Department's 2006 Religious Freedom Report cites two examples of such successful challenges.[242]

While anti-Christian violence is virtually unheard of in Israel, the rare incident does occur. The State Department describes a single incident, from February 2005, when Druze rioters "damaged a Melkite Catholic church and damaged or burned dozens of Christian-owned businesses, homes, and cars . . . after a Druze falsely claimed that Christian youths had placed pornographic pictures of Druze girls on the Internet." In March of the same year, vandals painted the phrase, "Death to Gentiles" on ten Christian graves in a Jerusalem cemetery.[243]

Asia

Indonesia

Indonesia is the home of the Muslim terrorist group, Jemaah Islamiyah. An attack carried out by the group in October 2005 killed 22 people and injured 100. Jemaah Islamiyah's ability to survive diligent government attempts to stamp it out is one sign that Indonesia's reputed tradition of religious tolerance may be changing. Another sign is a January 2006 survey in which 40 percent of Indonesia's Muslims expressed support for the stoning of adulterers. As in Europe (or "Eurabia," as some observers, including myself, increasingly call it), this trend toward Islamic conservatism may be due less to a change in heart by the native Muslim Indonesian population than to an influx of fundamentalist Muslim immigrants.[244]

In May 2005, a bomb killed 22 people and injured over 30 in the predominantly Christian town of Tentena.[245]

---

[242] Ibid.
[243] Ibid.
[244] "Indonesia—International Religious Freedom Report 2006, *Bureau of Democracy, Human Rights, and Labor,   U.S.   Department   of   State.*   Available   online   at   http://www.state .gov/g/drl/rls/irf/2006/71341.htm.
[245] Tim Johnston, "Three Indonesian girls beheaded," *BBC News*, October 29, 2005.

On October 21, 2005, "[a] man on a motorcycle fire[d] at a house used for prayer meetings by a Christian congregation, injuring the owner."[246]

On October 29, 2005, three girls were beheaded as they walked through a cocoa plantation on the way to school. "It is unclear what was behind the attack, but the girls attended a private Christian school and one of the heads was left outside a church leading to speculation that it might have had a religious motive."[247]

On December 31, 2005, a market selling pork was bombed, killing seven and injuring more than 50. Also, according to the Indonesian Christian Communication Forum, "militant groups" forced more than 34 churches to close. Some church leaders later claimed that they were threatened with "sticks and similar weapons." Police on the scene either did nothing or actively helped the attackers.[248]

On June 5, 2007, a mob of approximately 100 "Muslim hardliners" attacked a church and beat the pastor's wife, "smashing images of Jesus and demanding the church be closed." It was the latest in a series of church attacks, including one on this same church, in 2005.[249] The problem of "Muslim hardliners" forcing churches to close is especially serious in West Java, where more than 30 churches have been forced to close since September 2004.[250]

On August 13, 2007, 80,000 radical Muslims assembled in a Jakarta sports stadium "to call for the creation of a Muslim state spanning the Islamic world."[251]

According to the State Department's 2006 report on religious freedom in Indonesia, "Certain policies, laws, and

---

[246] "Indonesia—International Religious Freedom Report 2006."
[247] Tim Johnston.
[248] "Indonesia—International Religious Freedom Report 2006."
[249] "Islamist mob hits church," The Australian, June 5, 2007.
[250] "Indonesia—West Java: Another Christian Church Attacked," Asia News. Available online at http://www.asianews.it/index.php?1=en&art=9462&geo=21&size=A.
[251] In other words, the restoration of the Caliphate. Kathy Marks, "Islamists rally to demand creation of Muslim state," The Independent (London), August 13, 2007.

official actions restricted religious freedom, and the Government sometimes tolerated discrimination against and the abuse of religious groups by private actors."[252]

Malaysia

The Malaysian Government restricts sales in peninsular Malaysia of Christian tapes and other printed materials, and of Malay-language translations of the Bible, whose covers must display the legend, "Not for Muslims." The movie, "The Passion of the Christ," could only be screen privately, away from Muslims, who were forbidden to see it. The Government also "pressures" non-Muslims to wear headscarves; non-Muslim women must wear them for lectures and graduation ceremonies at the International Islamic University of Malaysia. All female police officers, whatever their religion, must wear headscarves.[253]

Reuters reports that, in recent times, the Malaysian government has demolished a number of churches and made it "difficult" for Christians to build new ones. State television broadcasts Islamic programs, but none for other faiths.[254]

In June 2007, two churches are attacked.[255]

On June 14, 2007. "Muslim extremist" demonstrators threatened to "close down churches operating in private homes." Three days later, a pastor received an anonymous letter "promising to destroy his home if it is 'still functioning as a church.'"[256] And of course, Malaysian Christians would not need to turn private homes into churches if Malaysian

[252] "Indonesia – International Religious Freedom Report 2006."
[253] "Malaysia – International Religious Freedom Report 2006, *Bureau of Democracy, Human Rights, and Labor,*   *U.S.   Department   of   State.*   Available   online   at http://www.state.gov/g/drl/rls/irf/2006/71347.htm.
[254] Liau Y-Sing, "Rise of Islam rankles Malaysia's minority faiths," *Reuters,* July 8, 2007.
[255] "Indonesia: Muslim Radicals Threaten House Churches," *Christian Persecution Info,* June 25, 2007. Available online at http://www.christianpersecution.info/news/Indonesia -muslim-radicals-threaten-house-churches.
[256] Ibid.

law did not make it so difficult to build a real one. To get a "worship permit" in Malaysia, a proposed church must:

- Prove it has at least 90 members,
- Get the consent of 60 neighbors of different faiths,
- Get the approval of local authorities and
- Get a separate building permit.[257].

In early September 2007, as Malaysia celebrated the 50th anniversary of its independence from Britain, Chief Justice Ahmad Fairuz called for the imposition of Shari'a law over the entire country.[258]

India

For whatever consolation it can offer decent, modern Muslims appalled at the pervasive persecution of Christians in so many Muslim-majority states, there is one non-Muslim country where Christians are persecuted: India. In India, uniquely, both Christians *and* Muslims are persecuted by India's majority faith, Hinduism. In its *International Religious Freedom Report 2006*, the State Department states that India's ultranationalist *Rashtriya Swayamsevak Singh* (RSS) party "has been implicated in incidents of violence and discrimination against Christians and Muslims."[259]

Media reports of Indian anti-Christian violence began to surface in 1997, with 24 incidents reported in just that one year, compared to a combined total of 38 incidents for the entire period, 1964 to 1996. By 1998, the number had risen to 90.[260] In 1999, Human Rights Watch reported "increasing violence against Christians," including "the killing of priests, the raping of nuns, and the physical destruction of Christian

[257] "Indonesia: Muslim Radicals Threaten House Churches."
[258] Thomas Bell, "Malyasia considers switch to Islamic law," *Daily Telegraph* (London), September 1, 2007.
[259] "India – International Religious Freedom Report 2006, *Bureau of Democracy, Human Rights, and Labor, U.S. Department of State*. Available online at http://www.state.gov/g/drl/rls/irf/2006/71440.htm.
[260] Vinay Lal, "Anti-Christian Violence in India," *Manas*, UCLA College of Letters and Science, (undated, but almost certainly 2000 or early 2001).

institutions, schools, churches, colleges and seminaries."[261]
The years since have brought no improvement.

On May 22, 2006, when members of the Indian
Evangelical Team Church refused an order by "a group of
Hindu extremists," one Christian was stoned. When
Christians complain to local authorities, they, not the
Hindus, were charged—with "desecrating a Hindu
goddess."[262]

On June 4, 2006, a Hindu mob, 50 strong, disrupted a
Christian prayer meeting, "accusing Pastor Jagdish Bharti of
destroying the Hindu religion and demanding that he
renounce his faith and worship the Hindu god Bajrang." The
mob then abducted all 25 members, taking them to a Hindu
temple where they were forced to "bow before the idols."
Female members were "threatened with rape if they should
continue attending Christian prayer meetings." Again,
instead of seeking out the Hindu attackers, police arrested 15
Christians, including Pastor Bharti, whom they charged with
the "'deliberate and malicious intention of outraging . . .
religious feelings."[263]

On June 8, 2006, a young man asked Pastor Kumar, a lay
preacher, to lead a prayer service. Hours later, the preacher's
body was found in a forest, his head so badly crushed that
he could be identified only by his clothing.[264]

On April 29, 2007, "extremists" from the Vishwa Hindu
Parishad (World Hindu Council) beat Pastor Walter Masih
"while a national television news channel filmed the
attack.[265]

On May 6, 2007, "Hindu extremists" invaded a Christian
home and threatened Pastor Than Singh John, his wife and

[261] "Anti-Christian Violence on the Rise in India," *Human Rights Watch*, September 30, 1999. Available online at http://hrw.org/English/docs/1999/09/30/india1626.htm.
[262] Ibid.
[263] Ibid.
[264] Ibid.
[265] "India: Attacks in Rajasthan State Show Disturbing Trend," *Compass Direct News*, May 24, 2007.

their two children, demanding that the family leave their village.[266]

On May 12, 2007, a Hindu mob ransacked the home of Father Paul Ninama, threatening to "burn him alive" if he did not leave the village of Parsad.[267]

On June 11, 2007, two Christians were murdered. One was stabbed five times; the other, an 86-year-old man, was stabbed 24 times.[268]

On October 27, 2007, four Christian youths, three of them girls, were arrested after the leader of a "Hindu extremist organization" accused them of forcibly converting Hindus.

On December 24, 2007, "[A]t least" six churches were torched and one person, a Hindu, killed in Hindu-Christian violence that required 450 police to put down. Each group blamed the other for starting the violence.

On December 29, 2007, a mob of 10 to 15 "Muslim extremists" demolished an "underground house church."[269]

The pretext for much of the Hindu violence is the allegation that Christians are forcibly converting Hindus, even though the Christians percentage of the Indian population actually is declining.[270] Conversely, according to Human Rights Watch, thousands of Christians have been forcibly converted to Hinduism.

The increased violence against India's Christians coincides with the 1998 rise to power of the ultra-nationalist *Baharatiya Janata* Party (BJP), one of India's two major parties (the other being the Congress Party). In a 1999 report, "Politics by Other Means: Attacks Against Christians in

---

[266] Ibid.
[267] Ibid.
[268] "India Christian Workers Murdered Amid Spreading Anti-Christian Violence," *BosNewsLife News Center*, June 12, 2007. Available online at http://www.worthynews .com/Christian/india-christian-workers-murdered-amid-spreading-anti-christian-violence/
[269] Michael Ireland, "House Church run by Salem Voice Ministries demolished by Muslim extremists," *Journal Chretien*, December 31, 2007. Available online at http://www.spcm.org/Journal/spip.php?breve6081.
[270] Vinay Lal.

India," Human Rights Watch described attacks on Christians in the months preceding and following the 1998 elections.[271]

The BJP promotes a "Hindu nationalist ideology"[272] that, like their ultra-nationalist fellow travelers in the RSS, views India as a "Hindu nation" and Hinduism as more than just a religion, but a complete way of life, in the same way that fundamentalist Muslims view Islam. It probably should not surprise us, then, that as the former persecutes the latter, the latter persecutes the former. For example, when members of the RSS and another "fundamentalist Hindu group," Vishwa Hindu Parishad (VHP) led "avenging Hindu mobs" on a rampage that resulted in "incidents of arson" and the death of one Muslim man, who was "burnt alive in his car," it was in retaliation for an earlier massacre, by Muslim militants, of 35 Hindus in Indian Kashmir on April 30 and May 1, 2006.[273]

Another phenomenon contributing to Hindu anti-Christian hostility in India is the same one that we have seen sparking Muslim hostility towards Christians in Judea, Samaria, Gaza and Lebanon:

> [R]ates of literacy among both Christian men and women are higher than among Hindu men and women, and in the various indices that are used internationally to determine social and economic development, such as infant mortality rate, maternal mortality rate, and death rate, Christians score better.[274]

The BJP, ousted in the most recent elections after a series of scandals, including a sex scandal that forced the party's general secretary to resign, is struggling to regain power. But

---

[271] Cited in "Anti-Christian Violence on the Rise in India."
[272] "India's BJP names new president," *BBC News,* January 2, 2006.
[273] "India: End Communal Violence in Gujarat, Kashmir," *Human Rights Watch,* May 4, 2006.
[274] Vinay Lal.

whichever party carries India's next election, I would not look for any dramatic increase in tolerance for her Christians.

Pakistan

U.S. cooperation with Pakistan against the Taliban and Al-Qaeda remnants that fled there after being routed in Afghanistan keeps India's neighbor in the news, but, sadly, only regarding the fight against Islamic terrorism. Garnering far less coverage is the plight of Pakistani Christians.

November 2005: Told that Christians were desecrating Korans, "a Muslim mob wielding axes and sticks set fire to three churches, a dozen houses, three schools, a dispensary, a convent and two parsonages?"[275]

In February 2006, a mob of 400 Muslims, hearing that "a local Christian had burned pages from the Koran," set fire to a church.[276]

No doubt, it is incidents such as these, along with the general discrimination and harassment Christian Pakistanis endure, that "inspire" many of them to convert to Islam. Certainly, it is not any attraction to the faith itself, if this report of one newly-converted family is any indication:

> A recent convert from Christianity to Islam, Bashir Masi knew nothing of his new faith.
>
> He could not describe a single tenet of Islam, nor remember the Qalma, the Muslim declaration of faith, nor name his own children, who have adopted Muslim names.
>
> He, his wife Anna and their six children converted to Islam 15 days ago. "We are happy

---

[275] Isambard Wilkinson, "Where Christianity faces a fight to survive," *Coalition for Responsible Peace in the Middle East* Website, http://c4rpme.org/bin/articles.cgi?Cat =Christians&Subcat=cmr&ID=393.
[276] Ibid.

now we are Muslim," said Mr. Masi. "It is a great religion."

The Masis' conversion is typical of the vulnerability of Christians in Pakistan, many of whom live under the threat of persecution, death and who have suffered waves of violence directed against them and their churches.[277]

But other Christian Pakistanis, unlike Bashir Masi, refuse to abandon their faith, even on pain of death. On May 7, 2007, Christians in the towns of Charsadda and Mardan received unsigned, handwritten letters giving them ten days to "close their churches and convert to Islam." Some of the letters threatened "bombing or the execution of all Christians" who did not comply. Some Christians fled, but others, such as Shahbaz Bhatti, head of the All Pakistan Minorities Alliance, stood fast, proclaiming: "We will not [change our religion] even if we have to die."[278]

On May 14, 2007, the Pakistani government proposed a new "apostasy law" under which a man who leaves Islam would be put to death, and a woman imprisoned for life or "until repentance occurs." The apostate's property would be awarded only to Muslim relatives and "they also lose custody to any minor children in their care and guardianship, including their biological children." The proposed law joins Pakistan's existing "blasphemy law" which, the Human Rights Commission of Pakistan notes, is "widely used to settle petty, personal disputes" and has harmed "many innocent persons through its misuse."[279]

---

[277] Ibid.
[278] "Written threats to Pakistani Christians: close churches and convert to Islam," *Barnabas Fund*, May 14, 2007. Available online at http://www.barnabasfund.org/news/archives/text.php?ID_news_items=285.
[279] "Pakistan Christian Converts Could Face Death Penalty for Leaving Islam,", *BosNewsLife*, May 14, 2007. Available online at http://www.bosnewslife.com/index .php?/window/list.newsPrint=2942.

On June 29, 2007, Pakistani lawyers investigated a report that as many as 30 men tortured and gang-raped a young Christian man—yes, *man*—for refusing to convert to Islam."[280]

On October 27, 2007, "[s]uspected pro-Taliban militants" kidnapped two Christian hospital just five months after a similar kidnapping from the same hospital and less than one month after Muslims stormed the New Apostolic Church. Islamist militants in Pakistan regularly threaten to kill Christian clerics in Southern Punjab's Khanewal district if they do not "embrace Islam and stop preaching Christianity."[281]

Africa

Algeria

On June 5, 2007, Algeria's government issued a regulation requiring "advance authorization from the regional governor" for "non-Muslim public religious events," which the governor may reject "if the event is judged to be a threat to public order."[282]

On December 31, 2007, Algerian legislators belonging to Islamic political party of Al-Nahda asked the government to slow down 'the activities of Christian missionaries in the country."[283]

Eritrea

The Department of State has labeled Eritrea a "Country of Particular Concern" for the third straight year. "It is

---

[280] "Man Sexually Assaulted in Pakistan After Refusing to Convert to Islam," *Christian Today*, June 29, 2007. Available online at http://www.christiantoday.com/article/man.sexually.assaulted.in.pakistan.after.refusing.to.convert.to.islam/11332.htm.

[281] "Two Christians kidnapped from a hospital in Pakistan," *The Times of India*, October 27, 2007.

[282] "New Regulations For Non-Muslim Religious Activities in Algeria," *Al-Quds Al-Arabi* (London), June 5, 2007. Cited by the Middle East Media Research Institute at http://www.thememriblog.org/blog_personal/en/1801.htm.

[283] "Algeria: Islamic MPs ask for action against Christian missionaries," *Adnkronos* (Algeria), December 31, 2007. Available online at http://www.adnkronos.com/AKI /English/Religion/?id=1.0.1721763459.

estimated that some 2,000 Christians are currently detained without trial or charge in Eritrea."[284]

In May 2007, authorities arrested 80 members of the Mehrete Yesus Evangelical Presbyterial Church in Asmara at the close of a Sunday worship service. "'They have been told not to teach or preach, but they haven't been asked to leave,'" said an anonymous source.[285]

In May 2007, the Eritrean government installed a new patriarch of the Eritrean Orthodox Tewhado Church and placed the former patriarch under house arrest after he criticized the government "for interfering in church activities and for persecuting evangelical churches."[286]

Nigeria

Chalk up another swath of destruction for the Danish Mohammed-cartoon fanatics. On February 20, 2006, 58 people were killed and 30 churches burned in "protests" over the cartoons.[287] One Christian "watched helplessly as six of his children were burnt to ashes." In addition Nigeria's *Daily Sun* newspaper counted "over 50 shops and three hotels ... burnt, looted or destroyed." The Christian Association of Nigeria accused the police of "complicity in the crisis."[288] According to the State Department, "As many as 50,000 persons were displaced and 150 killed" in "sectarian violence" over the cartoons.[289]

On February 21, 2006, the Red Cross recovered 13 bodies after machete-wielding youths burned two churches in a "sectarian riot." The riot erupted when a teacher's

---

[284] Ibid.

[285] "Eritrea: Authorities Arrest 80-Member Presbyterian Congregation," *Compass Direct News*, May 4, 2007.

[286] Ethan Cole, "Eritrea Installs Controversial New Orthodox Patriarch," *Christian Post*, May 29, 2007.

[287] This is the fourth time I have cited the "Danish cartoon incident" as the inspiration for Muslim anti-Christian violence. Has anyone calculated the total number of people killed, to date, over some #&%$@*! *cartoons?*

[288] "Maiduguri mayhem: 58 killed, 30 churches burnt," *Daily Sun* (Nigeria), February 20, 2006. Available online at http://odili.net/news/source/2006/feb/20/802.html.

[289] "Nigeria—International Religious Freedom Report 2006, *Bureau of Democracy, Human Rights, and Labor, U.S. Department of State.* Available online at http://www.state.gov/g/drl/rls/irf/2006/71318.htm.

confiscation of a Koran from a student turned into a rumor that the Koran was desecrated.[290]

On March 22, 2007, "[a]n angry mob of Muslim students" beat secondary teacher Oluwatoyin Olushekan to death after a student accused her of "tearing a portion of the Koran that she seized from a female student during an examination."[291]

In October 2007, a church in the "northern state of Borno" received three letters "warning that members would be attacked in the next few days."[292]

Sudan: "Welcome to Hell"

"Welcome to Hell" is the title of British reporter A.A. Gill's 2004 article that appeared in London's *Sunday Times*. But if Gill's reporting is to be believed, "hell" barely begins to describe what life is like for the Christians of the Sudan. In the article, Gill describes the Janjaweed, the "irregular bandit cavalry" that preys on the Christians[293], as

> the most feared and sadistically ruthless thugs on a continent glutted with horror. The Janjaweed come and kill all the men and boys. They rape the women and take some as slaves, burn the villages and the crops they can't steal.[294]

And what does the international community do? So far, nothing. The UN offers only talk and not a single majority-Christian has stepped forward to offer to grant asylum to the suffering Christians of the Sudan, or of Darfur — precisely why I feel so strongly that there must be a Christian-state

---

[290] "Curfew after third Nigerian riot," *BBC News*, February 21, 2006. Available online at http://news.bbc.co.uk/1/hi/world/Africa/4735014.stm.

[291] "Teacher murdered over holy Quaran 'desecration,'" *Daily Times* (Pakistan), March 22, 2007.

[292] "Nigeria: Muslim Threat to Attack Church Raises Tensions," October 10, 2007. Available online at http://compassdirect.org/en/display.php?page=news&length=short&lang=en &idelement=5069.

[293] And on black Muslims as well — as good an example as any, except the *60-year* confinement of Muslim refugees to camps — of the obvious, but all-too-little-acknowledged fact that no one is crueler to Muslims than other Muslims.

[294] A.A. Gill, "Welcome to hell," *Sunday Times* (London), July 11, 2004.

version of Israel, with an Israel-style right of return, that *will* take them in.

Indeed—and interestingly (and perhaps ironically)—one of the countries that *does* grant asylum to Sudanese Christians is—yes—Israel. As of July 2007, Israel had taken in 2,400 Christian refugees from the Sudan—and from Eritrea, Ghana, and Kenya as well—with "dozens more arriving every day."[295] It is equally interesting to note that, to get to the Jewish state, Sudanese Christians must pass through a Muslim one, Egypt. But they have no desire to *remain* there—and once out, they are desperate to *stay* out. Anthony Peter, a Christian Sudanese who entered Israel illegally from Egypt, explains why:

> "I would rather that the Israeli government shoot me here, in a clean, humane way, than send me back to Egypt. To send me, and my children, and my wife back there is to sentence us to a cruel and violent death.
>
> "My life in Egypt was *even more dangerous than my life in Sudan* had been. Our lives were even more at risk and we were outsiders who everyone could identify and threaten."
>
> Peter said he had seen other Sudanese refugees beaten, raped and killed by Nubian gangs operating in the refugee camps.
>
> "I had to bribe them with a quarter of my wages each week to keep my family safe. I had to tell my wife and children to never leave the house, to always be afraid."

[295] Sheera Claire Frenkel, Ilana Diamond and staff, "Sudanese allowed to stay—for now," *Jerusalem Post*, July 8, 2007.

Peter even tried to return to Sudan, but was turned away at the border.

"I quickly realized that this new place was even more dangerous than Sudan had been. But they would not let me return."

So Peter decided to take a gamble on Israel, a place he had only heard of as the "land of Jews."

"The only thing I knew about Jews was what I heard about them in Egypt—that they were evil, that they drank blood and were killers and very cruel. I thought though, that the people telling me this were also killers, so why should I believe them?"[296]

Fortunately, for Peter, he did *not* believe them, came to Israel and learned what Muslim Palestinians would—and in fact, did, during the 20 years that Israel administered Judea, Samaria and Gaza: that everything they have been taught about Jews—specifically, how Jews treat non-Jews—is wrong.

But as Peter's statement indicates, reaching Israel and being able to stay there are two different things. There are, sadly, literally millions of refugees and Israel is a small country. Lamented Yossef Amnon, a spokesman for the city of Beersheba:

We have reached the saturation point and can no longer provide shelter or food for the refugees. The government has repeatedly promised to act, but they have not. The city's resources and the resources of the charitable

---

[296] Sheera Claire Frankel, "Refugee flees Sudan for Israel, despite rumors," *Jerusalem Post*, July 2, 2007. (emphases added)

students and volunteers in the area are exhausted.

Thus, the Israeli government, reluctantly, is preparing to send all but the most serious cases back to Egypt, whose president, Hosni Mubarak, notwithstanding the fears expressed by refugees such as Anthony Peter, has promised to protect them, or to friendly African countries, such as Ghana or Kenya.[297]

I dwell on Peter's story at such length because it so well exemplifies the dichotomy that so torments the world's persecuted Christians: a desperate need to leave, the grievous absence of a place to which to go.

On November 30, 2007, "[t]housands of Sudanese, many armed with clubs and swords and beating drums, burned pictures of a British teacher Friday and demanded her execution for insulting Islam by letting her students name a teddy bear Mohammed."[298]

Around the World

According to Britain's *Sunday Express,* in 2007, the British Secret Service, MI6, estimated that "some 200 million Christians in 60 countries ... are at risk of suffering persecution."[299] Open Doors, a Christian Human Rights organization, publishes an annual list of the world's top 50 worst persecutors of Christians. Here is their list for 2007:[300]

World's Top 50 Worst
Persecutors Of Christians

1. North Korea	26. Libya
2. Saudi Arabia	27. Nigeria (North)
3. Iran	28. Djibouti

[297] Sheera Claire Frenkel, "Gov't eyes Ghana, Kenya as possible havens for refugees," *Jerusalem Post,* October 18, 2007.
[298] Mohamed Osman, "Teacher Hidden As Sudan Mob Urges Death," *AP,* November 30, 2007.
[299] "200 million Christians in 60 countries subject to persecution," *Catholic News Agency,* June 19, 2007.
[300] "World Watch List prayer profiles," *Open Doors,* http://www.opendoorsuk.org/wwl _profiles/intro.php

4. Somalia

5. Maldives

6. Yemen

7. Bhutan

8. Vietnam

9. Laos

10. Afghanistan

11. Uzbekistan

12. China

13. Eritrea

14. Turkmenistan

15. Comoros

16. Chechnya

17. Pakistan

18. Egypt

19. Myanmar

20. Sudan

21. Iraq

22. Azerbaijan

23. Brunei

24. Cuba

25. Qatar

29. India

30. Sri Lanka

31. Algeria

32. Mauritania

33. Morocco

34. Tajikistan

35. Turkey

36. Oman

37. Ethiopia

38. United Arab Emirates

39. Kuwait

40. Jordan

41. Indonesia

42. Belarus

43. Colombia

44. Bangladesh

45. Syria

46. Tunisia

47. Kenya (North-East)

48. Nepal

49. Mexico (South)

50. Bahrain

PERSECUTION OF CHRISTIAN CONVERTS

As badly as born Christians are persecuted in many countries, those who are not born to the faith, but come to it from Islam or (in the case of India) Hinduism, are treated even worse—so much worse, that the plight of the Christian convert deserves to be examined, country-by-country, in it's own chapter.

Afghanistan

In a case that made headlines worldwide, only pressure from the international community and Afghan president Hamid Karzai's personal intervention prevented the execution of Afghan Christian convert Abdul Rahman.[1] This happened *after* Afghanistan's liberation from the Islamo-tyranny of the Taliban (at, I might add, the cost of much U.S. treasure and many American lives). Needless to say, had the Taliban still been running things, Rahman's fate would have been considerably different.

Egypt

In the mid-1990s, under pressure from the rising Islamic fundamentalism described earlier,[2] Egypt reintroduced the *hadit*—sayings of Mohammed used to interpret the Koran. One hadit holds that "the blood of a Muslim 'may be spilled in three cases: homicide, adultery, and apostasy.'"[3] As Youssef Sidhom, director of the Christian weekly, *Watani*, explains:

---

[1] "Afghan president intervenes in case of Christian convert," *Sydney Morning Herald* (Australia), March 26, 2006.
[2] See the section on Egypt, beginning on page 41.
[3] Dina Nascetti, "Thou Shalt Have No Other Allah," *L'espresso* (Italy), December 5-11, 2003.

> A Muslim from birth can never change religions.
> [Other Muslims] will not only seek by every
> means to dissuade him, but *his very life will be in
> danger*. He will be excluded from his inheritance
> and from the community to which he belongs.
> But on the contrary, an Egyptian Christian who
> embraces the Muslim faith is welcomed with
> many parties, his identity card is quickly
> changed, he is helped in his job and with his
> house.[4]

Egyptian law does not "provide a legal means for
converts from Islam to Christianity to amend their civil
records to reflect their new religious status,"[5] as one
unfortunate Egyptian convert discovered when he tried to
amend his. On August 2, 2007, Mohammed Ahmed Hegazy,
25 at the time and a Christian convert since age 16, became
the first convert to file a lawsuit against Egypt's interior
ministry "for rejecting his application to replace Islam with
Christianity on his identification papers." As with the
Turkish headscarf ban, this is no trivial issue. For example,
because Ahmed currently remains legally Muslim despite
his conversion, he was forced to marry his bride, Zeinab, in
an Islamic wedding. Now Zeinab is pregnant and the
Hegazys want their child to be born into their faith;
however, if Ahmed and Zeinab remain legally Muslim, their
child will be legally Muslim and unable to "enroll in
Christian religious classes at school, marry in a church [or]
attend church services openly."

The Hegazys' desire to choose their religion and to
practice it freely has not sat well with the Muslim
community, which has "[retaliated by filing a lawsuit and

---

[4] Quoted in Dina Nascetti. (emphasis added)
[5] "Egypt—International Religious Freedom Report 2006."

delivering death threats against his lawyer."[6] Death threats, from "Muslim fanatics," against the Hegazys themselves have forced the Hegazys into hiding, unable even to attend their own court hearing. "It's like we are in prison and have no way out," says Hegazy.[7] Yet, even in the face of such ardent opposition, including death threats, Hegazy's faith remained strong as did his resolve to fight for the right to choose his religion, and to have his government respect that choice: "I put my trust in God, and I feel I need to persevere. . . . "This is my duty to myself, my family, all Muslims who converted to Christianity, and all Christians."[8]

I would have liked to have reported a happy resolution of Hegazy's case, but, sadly, on January 29, 2008, a Cairo court ruled against Hegazy. In doing so, the court cited

> Article II of the Egyptian constitution, which makes Islamic law, or *sharia*, the source of Egyptian law. The judge said that, according to sharia, Islam is the final and most complete religion and therefore Muslims already practice full freedom of religion and cannot return to an older belief (Christianity or Judaism).

"He can believe whatever he wants in his heart," said Judge Muhammad Husseini, "but on paper he can't convert." According to Hegazy's lawyer, "The judge didn't listen to our defense and we didn't even have a chance to talk before the court." Hegazy plans to appeal the ruling or open a new case if possible. "Hegazy's wife Zeinab, also a convert from Islam, plans to go to court for her right to register as a Christian as well."[9] A recent decision by an

---

[6] "Christian Convert Sues Egypt Over Legal Status," *Assyrian International News Agency*, August 9, 2007, http:www.aina.org/news/2007089102345.htm. Citing *Compass Direct News*.
[7] "Egypt: Islamists Join case Against Convert to Christianity," *Compass Direct News*, October 10, 2007. Available online at http://compassdirect.org/en/display.php ?page=news &length=short&lang=en&idelement=5069.
[8] Ibid. (emphasis added)
[9] "Egypt: Court Rules Against Convert," *Compass Direct News*, January 31, 2008. Available online at http://www.compassdirect.org/en/display.php?page=lead&lang =en&length=long&idelement=&backpage=&critere=&countryname=&rowcur=

Egyptian court to recognize the conversions of 12 Egyptians to Christianity will not help the Hegazys because all 12 of the conversions were actually "re-conversions" of born Christians who had converted to Islam and wished to reclaim their former faith. "The judge ruled that the 12 would not be considered apostates because they were born Christian [but] the ruling . . . does not apply to converts who were born Muslim." Interestingly, most of the defendants were represented by Hegazy's lawyer, Ramsis Raouf El-Naggar. "We're working on his case because we want to have freedom of religion in Egypt."[10]

Muslim Egyptians who convert to Christianity and try to have their conversions recognized on their identity cards have been arrested for "falsifying documents." Some have been "interrogated and physically abused in an attempt to obtain information on other converts and their activities."[11]

Converts, if their conversion becomes known publicly, can expect to be pressured, sometimes severely, to recant. Christian convert Bahaa el-Akkad was imprisoned for two years without ever being officially charged with a crime. El-Akkad finally regained his freedom on April 28, 2007, only hours after being threatened with an additional *ten* years' imprisonment if he did not recant. To which threat, according to Akkad's lawyer, Akkad calmly responded, "God has brought me to this place, and He alone will let me go to my home. You cannot do anything against God." Akkad remains free, but reportedly under continuous observation—and threat from the Muslim Brotherhood, who have vowed to kill him.[12]

What recourse, then, do Egyptian Christian converts have when the courts abandon them, the police oppress them and

---

[10] Rachelle Kliger, "Egypt recognizes Christian converts," *The Media Line News Agency, Jerusalem Post,* February 10, 2008.
[11] "Egypt—International Religious Freedom Report 2006"
[12] "Egypt—Jailed Christian Convert Released," May 25, 2007, *Open Doors UK.* Available online at http://www .opendoorsuk.org.uk/news/news_archives/001905.php.s

their neighbors and even members of their own family shun and even threaten to kill them? Says one Egyptian priest:

> Assuming they are not condemned, the only thing they can do is to go into exile in the United States, Canada or Australia, in order to avoid disdain both within their families and in the communities around them.

Actually, Christian converts have one more choice: They can remain in Egypt and practice their new faith secretly. "Ibrahim" is a practicing Muslim – but only in public. In his private life, and in his heart, "Ibrahim" has long been Mikeil, the Christian name he adopted when he converted – a conversion so secret that "[h]is family, his friends and even his wife are unaware of it." If they ever do become aware of it and expose him, Ibrahim/Mikeil risks "a death sentence, or in the best of cases a sentence which would inflict years of imprisonment and certain torture."[13]

England

Yes, England. Nowadays, even Christian converts in Western, modern, supposedly enlightened Europe are not safe, for as England's Muslim population has grown, so, too, has the danger to Muslim apostates. Nowhere is the problem more serious than in England, where the persecution of Muslim apostates is becoming increasingly serious – and common. Maryam Namazi, of the Council of Ex-Muslims of Britain believes that many so-called honor killings (another practice on the rise in England) "are actually murders of people who have renounced Islam."[14]

One female Muslim apostate tells how her family, including her "kind loving father," turned on her after she converted to Christianity:

---

[13] Dina Nascetti.
[14] Alasdair Palmer, "Muslim apostates threatened over Christianity," *Daily Telegraph* (London), December 10, 2007.

He said he couldn't have me in the house now that I was a Kaffir [an insulting term for a non-Muslim]. . . .

He said I was damned for ever. He insulted me horribly. I couldn't recognize that man as the father who had been so kind to me as I was growing up.

My mother's transformation was even worse. She constantly beat me about the head. She screamed at me all the time. I remember saying to them, *as they were shouting death threats*, "Mum, Dad—you're saying you should kill me . . . but I'm your daughter! Don't you realise that?"

* * *

They put their loyalty to Islam above any love for me."[15]

And no, let me remind you once again, we are not talking about Saudi Arabia or Pakistan. We are talking about *England*:

It was such a shock. I remember thinking *when they brought all my uncles round to try to intimidate me*—all these men were lined up telling me how terrible a person I was, how the devil had taken me—I remember thinking, how can this be happening? *Because this isn't Lahore in Pakistan. This is Degenham in London! This is Britain!*[16]

Welcome, then, to the new England and her capital, Lahore on the Thames. Former prime minister Tony Blair's "Cool Britannia" is quickly becoming "Cruel Britannia," at least for Christian converts from Islam. "Hanna" (not her real name), a "British imam's daughter, is living in fear of

---

[15] Ibid. (emphasis added)
[16] Ibid. (emphasis added)

her life under police protection after receiving death threats from her family for converting to Christianity."[17]

India

In my earlier discussion of India,[18] I mentioned the country's two Hindu nationalist parties, the BJP and the RSS. Both are hardliners on the matter of converts, but, as the State Department notes, "the RSS in particular oppose[s] conversions from Hinduism and believe[s] that all citizens, regardless of their religious affiliation, should adhere to Hindu cultural values."[19] This rising "Hindu nationalism," in two major Indian political parties, bodes ill for India's Christians, as does another phenomenon: the disparity of treatment between new and old converts. According to a University of California study,

> recent converts to Christianity fare much worse than those Indian Christians who have been members of that faith for one or more generations. Recent converts are seen as traitors to Hinduism, as people who are against the tide of history and fail to recognize that India is—as the Hindu militants would like to think—a Hindu nation.[20]

On May 1, 2006, on learning that a Hindu woman converted to Christianity, her husband demanded that she recant and when she refused, evicted her. They then burned down the church of the pastor who allegedly performed the conversion.[21]

---

[17] Ruth Gledhill, "British imam's daughter under police protection after converting to Christianity," *The Times* (London), December 5, 2007.

[18] Beginning on page 83.

[19] "India—International Religious Freedom Report 2006."

[20] Vinay Lal.

[21] "Anti-Christian Violence in India," *The Milli Gazette Online*, September 8, 2006. Available online at http://www.milligazette.com/dailyupdate/2006/20060908_Anti _Christian_Violence_India_terrorism.htm

Iran

In 2004, authorities raided the Assemblies of God's annual conference, arresting 80 religious leaders. Most were released the same day, with orders to stop meeting and to "stop talking about Jesus." One who was not, was Pastor Hamid Pourmand, a Muslim convert to Christianity for 25 years. Pastor Pourmand, along with his wife and two teenage children, was held for six weeks. The government then charged Pourmand, who was also a noncommissioned army officer, with espionage and moved him to a military prison. In 2005, a military court convicted Pourmand and sentenced him to three years imprisonment. He also faced automatic discharge from the army and forfeiture of his entire income, pension and housing for his family. Next, a civilian court tried him for "apostasy and proselytizing." The court acquitted Pourmand of these new charges and returned him to prison to serve out the rest of his espionage sentence.[22] But believe it or not, Pourmand actually got off lucky. According to the State Department, in Iran, "Apostasy, specifically conversion from Islam, may be punishable by death."

On November 22, 2005, after Christian convert Ghorban Tori was murdered, Iranian authorities searched his house "for Bibles and banned Christian books in Persian."

On May 2, 2006, after "several years of surveillance", authorities arrested Christian convert Ali Kaboli and give him the choice of being prosecuted for his conversion or leaving the country.[23]

Jordan

In Jordan, as in many Muslim countries, the various religious communities usually handle their own "social matters," such as marriage and divorce. But not converts

---

[22] "Iran—International Religious Freedom Report 2006."
[23] Ibid.

from Islam, who remain legally Muslim "in matters of family and property law"[24] and continue to be judged by Jordan's Shari'a courts, according to Islamic law. This, in a classic Catch-22, includes the law against leaving Islam, as one convert found out:

> The [Shari'a court's] verdict declared the convert to be a ward of the state, stripped him of his civil rights, and annulled his marriage. It further declared him to be without any religious identity. It stated that he lost all rights of inheritance and may not remarry his (now former) wife unless he returns to Islam, and forbade his being considered an adherent of any other religion. The verdict implies the possibility that legal and physical custody of his child could be assigned to someone else. The convert reportedly left the country with his family . . .[25]

In 2002, a Jordanian court awarded custody of a Christian woman's Christian children to the woman's brother-in-law based on an allegation that her deceased husband had converted to Islam shortly before his death, despite the widow's insistence that the husband's signature on the conversion certificate had been forged. The woman appealed and, in 2005, finally managed to get her children back, but only because she was able to show that her brother-in-law was mistreating the children.[26]

On April 14, 2006 the brother of a Christian convert agreed to drop his apostasy complaint only "after the convert's wife renounced in the presence of a lawyer any

24 "Jordan — International Religious Freedom Report 2006."
25 Ibid.
26 Ibid.

claims she might have to an inheritance from her own parents."[27]

Malaysia

The same kind of identity card requirement that makes life so difficult for Christian Egyptians afflicts Malaysia's Christians, too. In 2007, in a case that—a rarity in cases of Christian persecution—actually attracted the world's attention, 42-year old Lina Joy, a Christian convert from Islam since the age of 26, wished to marry a Christian man, but could not do so as long as her identity card continued to list her "legal" faith as Islam. (Remember, Shari'a forbids a Muslim woman to marry a non-Muslim man.) When Joy sought permission from a civilian court to remove "Islam" from her identity papers, the court ruled that it had no jurisdiction and that an Islamic court should decide the issue. But Malaysian Shari'a courts send apostates to counseling and, if they persist in their apostasy, fine or imprison them."[28] Since to appeal to the Shari'a court would be to expose herself as an apostate, subject to imprisonment and "Islamic counseling," Lina Joy cannot appeal at all. And so, she remains unmarried and in limbo.[29]

In the northern part of Malaysia, as of July 4, 2007, conversion from Islam is punishable by five years imprisonment and a $3,000 fine. Conversely, "[a] Malaysian Muslim who marries a non-Muslim and gets the non-Muslim to convert is rewarded with an apartment, a car, a one-time payment of $2,700, and a monthly stipend of $270."[30]

On February 5, 2008, Bishop Tan, president of the Christian Federation of Malaysia asked the government to

---

[27] Ibid.
[28] Jalil Hamid and Syed Azman, "Malaysia's Lina Joy loses Islam conversion case, *Boston Globe*, May 30, 2007.
[29] Ibid.
[30] "Malaysia adds to penalties for conversion from Islam," *Catholic World News*, July 4, 2007. Available online at http://www.cwnews.com/news/viewstory.cfm?recnum =52177.

"outlaw the confiscation of religious material" after 32 Bibles are confiscated at an airport by a "client services employee." "We have received many complaints from Christians being told to hand over religious books at various checkpoints in the country," says Tan.[31]

Morocco

A Moroccan man who married an Italian woman and converted from Islam to Christianity required hospitalization after being beaten by Muslims.

Nigeria

On October 9, 2007, an Islamic court awarded custody of Christian convert Allabe Kaku Chibok's three daughters to his deceased Muslim wife's relatives. A Muslim when they married, Chibok's wife divorced him when he converted, as Shari'a requires. "Islamic lawyers" had demanded that custody of the children be granted to the relatives because "under Islamic law the girls were now Muslims and could not be allowed to live with their Christian father."[32] (Remember: Under Shari'a, a Christian cannot "rule over" a Muslim.)

Pakistan

Pakistan recently introduced a law decreeing death for male apostates and, for females, imprisonment until they recant or for life if they do not.

Turkey

Annette Grossbongardt, a reporter for Germany's *Der Spiegel* magazine writes: "One of the most difficult positions is that of Turkish converts who turn their backs on the 'true faith.'"[33] According to the State Department's *International*

[31] MALAYSIA: Christians: "The government must clearly outlaw the confiscation of religious material," *Asia News*, February 5, 2008. Available online at http://www.asianews.it/index.php?1=en&art=11438&size=A.
[32] "Nigeria: Islamic Court Endorses Abduction of Girls," *Compass Direct News*, October 9, 2007. Available online at http://compassdirect.org/en/display.php?page =news&length =short&lang=en&idelement=5068.
[33] Annette Grossbongardt.

Religious Freedom Report 2006, local officials have harassed converts from Islam who sought to change the religious designation on their identity cards[34] and in 2003, Yakup Cindilli, a Christian convert, was beaten by "three members of the Nationalist Movement Party . . . for distributing New Testaments."[35]

Modern Turkey was conceived, at the outset, as a secular state[36] and indeed, according to one convert, the threat to Turkey's Christians—and Christian converts—comes not from the resolutely secular national government,[37] but from a minority of intolerant Turkish citizens. "Society is our problem, not the laws," says sociologist and Christian convert Behnan Konutgan.[38]

Israel

Christian converts, like born Christians, are not persecuted in Israel.[39]

---

[34] "Turkey—International Religious Freedom Report 2006."
[35] Ibid.
[36] See my earlier section on Turkey, beginning on page 73.
[37] Though, again, that may be about to change. See page 74.
[38] Annette Grossbongardt.
[39] "'Rabbis told Jews to shun Evangelicals,'" *Jerusalem Post* (via *AP*), September 24, 2007.

Having now seen ample evidence of the privations, discrimination and persecution Christians suffer—and will continue to suffer if nothing is done—we can proceed to my argument, which is twofold:

(1) Christians, especially those in the Middle East, must have *their own state*; and

(2) A Christian Middle Eastern state is *achievable*.

The Pragmatic Case

Aside from the occasional mention of Sudan or Darfur, when was the last time any leader, of any country, publicly deplored the persecution of Christians? Apparently, the military intervention that brought the blessings of liberty to 50 million Afghanis and Iraqis will not be coming to the Christians of Darfur, Sudan or any of the countries in which Christians are persecuted, anytime soon.

In 1997, the Senate refused even to consider a bill, already passed by the House, that would have mandated automatic severe economic and political sanctions on any country adjudged to be guilty of religious discrimination. The Senate rejected the bill on two grounds. One was "the fear that sanctions ... would result in a backlash against the minorities the bill was intended to protect." But where was the fear of a "backlash" against black South Africans when the international community united against Apartheid?. And using the same logic, should Ronald Reagan not have kept silent about the plight of Soviet Jewry?

The second ground, that the bill "would make it impossible for the U.S. to put national security and trade concerns ahead of fighting religious persecution,"[1] does, admittedly, have some merit: Unless and until we develop a technology to drastically reduce our use of fossil fuels, there is little chance of imposing economic sanctions on, say, Saudi Arabia. But could the Senate not, at least, have passed a more limited bill covering only Samaria, Judea and Gaza, or any number of Christian-persecuting countries where the U.S. has no compelling economic interests?

From where I sit,[2] both grounds are canards. The real, unstated, reason why the Senate, the House, the President, the UN — virtually the entire international community — buries the plight of persecuted Christians is that to put the spotlight on what is being done to the Christians of Judea, Samaria and Gaza would be to expose, as well, who is doing it: the Muslim majority. That in turn, would threaten the international community's precious shibboleth, the "two-state solution," by raising the obvious, uncomfortable question: If this is how Muslim Palestinians are treat their Christian minority (and would be treat Jews, if they could[3]), what will happen to them if the Muslims are given *their own state* and, satisfied with having given them that state, the international community heaves a collective sigh of relief, turns its back and walks away? Not, of course, that the world is paying overly much attention even now.

Exposing Muslim Palestinians' "religious cleansing" of Judea, Samaria and Gaza, and the resultant devastating reduction of the Christian population also invites damning comparisons with Israel, whose Christian population, unlike

---

[1] Tony Carnes, "Religious Persecution Bill Drops Trade Sanction Clause," *Christianity Today*, April 27, 1998. Cited by Weiner, 32.

[2] A coffee house on East 86th Street, in Manhattan, in case you were wondering.

[3] And of course, the reason they cannot is because Jewish Palestinians, unlike their Christian counterparts, are safely ensconced *in their own state*, with a powerful Jewish army to defend it. Only when Christian Palestinians have the same, will they truly be safe; that is why I wrote this book.

those of Judea, Samaria and Gaza, which are declining, has almost *tripled* since the nation's 1948 re-founding. No, for the international community, nothing, not even the transformation of Bethlehem into a town with, as Bethlehem's late mayor, Elias Freij famously predicted, "churches but no Christians," must interfere with the "crusade" to add yet another Middle Eastern Muslim state to the 22 already there.

Even some evangelical, left wing Christians have hopped onto the appeasement bandwagon. On July 29, 2007, 34 such U.S. evangelical Christians published an open letter to President George W. Bush in the *New York Times*, urging progress on the two-state solution. The letter encouraged Bush not to "grow weary" in pursuing a "lasting peace," which is a fine sentiment—who doesn't want lasting peace?—but absurd as regards the region's Christians, for whom the only "peace" the two-state solution offers is the one the dinosaurs achieved: total extinction. I cannot imagine any statement more naïve than the one with which the 34 evangelicals ended their letter: "We renew our prayers and support for your leadership . . . and justice and peace for all the people in the Holy Land."[4]

Perhaps these Evangelicals for Appeasement will someday explain how giving Muslim Palestinians their own state in which to continue their ongoing persecution of the Christian minority with impunity will promote "justice and peace" for *Christians*. In the meantime, all their letter does is prove that none of its signatories actually live in Judea, Samaria or Gaza, because the views expressed therein differ so starkly from those expressed by Christians who *do* live there, as Yoram Ettinger relates:

---

[4] Letter cited in "Evangelicals' letter backs PA state," *Jerusalem Post*, July 29, 2007.

> Since the 1993 signing of the Oslo Accords, until the 1995 transfer of Bethlehem to the [Palestinian Liberation Organization], Palestinian Christians lobbied Israel *against the transfer*. The late Christian mayor, Elias Freij, warned that it would result in Bethlehem becoming a town with churches but no Christians. He lobbied Israel to include Bethlehem in the boundaries of Greater Jerusalem, as was the Jordanian practice until 1967.[5]

And here is another group of Christian Palestinians who appear far less eager to live under Fatah and Hamas than the outsiders who signed the *Times* letter are to put them there:

> On July 17, 2000, upon realizing that then [Israeli] Prime Minister Barak recklessly proposed the repartitioning of Jerusalem, the leaders of the Greek-Orthodox, Latin and Armenian Churches sent a letter to Clinton, Barak and Arafat, demanding to be consulted before such action was undertaken. Barak's proposal triggered a flood of requests for Israeli ID cards by East Jerusalem Arabs, who dreaded the PLO's aggressive track record.[6]

Which, of course, has been the problem all along: Christians are *never* consulted, *never* invited to participate in negotiations, about *anything* concerning their own future. And so, here we are, in 2008, as rumors surface, once again, that Israel might cede part of Jerusalem to the Palestinian Authority. Needless to say, "the flood of requests for Israeli ID cards by East Jerusalem Arabs," has resumed. Nor are the

---

[5] Yoram Ettinger. (emphasis added)
[6] Ibid.

requests coming only from Christians.[7] As we will see presently, the last thing *Muslim* Israelis want is to be placed under "Palestinian" rule.

Oslo Syndrome

No who has read this far can harbor any doubt about how bad life would be for Christian Judeans, Samarians and Gazans, were Israel's two former provinces and Egypt's former possession-by-conquest to be turned into a majority-Muslim "Palestinian state." Now consider also that:

- There never was a sovereign county, anywhere, anytime, called "Palestine;"
- There were no "Palestinians" in Judea, Samaria or Gaza before 1973. (UN Resolution 242, the original basis for a "Middle East peace," lacks even a single reference to "Palestinians," referring, instead, only to "refugees");
- Any Palestinian entity would remain, as Judea, Samaria and Gaza are today, economically dependent on Israel;
- Muslim Palestinians remain committed to a "one-state" solution—the replacement of Israel and the Palestinian territories with a single, Muslim state;[8] and
- A Muslim-dominated Palestinian state, assuming it includes Hamas, quickly would become (as Gaza already has) a jihadist recruiting center and training camp, with

---

[7] "More Jerusalem Arabs seek Israeli ID," *Jerusalem Post*, November 7, 2007.

[8] And while we're on the subject, why do single-state proponents oppose the expansion and addition of Israeli settlements? As long as no current Arab inhabitant is displaced, and, bit by bit, the land is annexed to Israel until the whole becomes a single state, and the overwhelming historical evidence that the Muslim (and Christian) inhabitants would be freer and more prosperous than they would in a majority-Muslim Middle Eastern state, what is their ground for objection? That Jews would be the majority should be immaterial—unless, of course, the goal is not a single state, but a *majority-Muslim* single state, in which case, those who call for a single state should be required, explicitly, to say so.

implications, including physical threats, reaching far beyond the Middle East.

Given all the above, why would anyone other than jihadists, anti-Zionists, anti-Semites and the clinically insane propose to do what, for all practical purposes, amounts to nothing more than taking one of the most lawless, dysfunctional places on earth and conferring on it the legitimacy of a "state?" And yet, the international community seems hell-bent on doing just that. Even more puzzling, so are many Israelis. Again, why?

Dr. Kenneth Levin, a clinical instructor of psychiatry at Harvard Medical School wondered, too, and thinks he has the answer, which he whimsically has named, "Oslo Syndrome," after Stockholm Syndrome, the phenomenon observed in some hostage situations, where the hostages, illogically, come to sympathize with their captors. Oslo, of course, is where the 1993 Oslo Accords were signed and which brought the terrorist Arafat, and his cronies out of virtual exile in distant Tunisia, and plunked them down in Judea, Samaria and Israel, *right next door*.

Everybody involved in the negotiations on the Israeli side (and indeed, the Palestinian side) should have predicted the result of giving Arafat and his band of bloodthirsty terrorists fanatically dedicated to Israel's destruction a more convenient location from which to attack her. Many did, and bitterly opposed the accords, but their warnings drowned in the enthusiasm of a lot of other, otherwise very smart, people who managed to delude themselves into believing that making it easier for Arafat to wage war would, somehow, paradoxically, inspire him to make peace. Even more astounding, most of these same people, despite everything that has happened since—the kidnappings, the suicide bombings, the Qassam rockets falling on southern

Israel daily—continue to believe this and remain as dedicated the two-state solution as ever.

In Europe's case, that's all right; after all, no one expects Frenchmen and Spaniards to act rationally.[9] But what puzzled Dr. Levin was the number of successive *Israeli* leaders who repeatedly pursued, and continue to pursue, against all common sense, a "peace process" that has, repeatedly, brought Israel nothing but *tsuris*.   (That's Yiddish for "trouble."):

> It was obvious to me at the start, as it was to many others, that the Oslo agreements could only lead to disaster. ... That there was something very deluded about the thinking of Israel's leaders and their pro-Oslo constituency became more evident as Oslo proceeded. Arafat and his Palestinian Authority immediately used their media, mosques and schools to promote hatred of Israel and violence against Jews and continued to make clear their objective remained Israel's destruction. The level of terrorism increased to unprecedented dimensions. *Yet Israel responded with more concessions.*
>
> During this period, there were many cogent critiques of the Oslo process. But none addressed *why* Israel's leaders, supported by the nation's academic and cultural elites and much of the broader population, were pursuing a course that was *demonstrably placing the nation, including their own families, at dire risk.* It seemed to me then, as it does now, that, given the

---

[9] In France's case, of course, Exhibit A is the French Revolution, but in more recent times, she proposed to lower unemployment by mandating a 35-hour workweek. Spaniard recently extended the rights normally accorded only to us humans, to apes.

irrationality of Israel's course, *the explanation had to lie in the realm of psychopathology.*

So what, exactly, is Oslo Syndrome? Referring to Israelis as a "population under chronic siege," Dr. Levin explains:

> [W]ithin populations under chronic siege — whether minorities marginalized, demeaned and attacked by surrounding societies or small nations besieged by their neighbors — some will invariably seek either to avert their gaze from the severity of the threat or rationalize the threat and blame themselves or others within their community for the danger. Their doing so reflects wishful thinking that if only they would reform sufficiently the danger would be alleviated.
>
> Israel has, at best, a capacity to respond effectively to attacks by its neighbors; it does *not* have the capacity to end the Arab siege, to force peace upon the Arabs. Peace, if and when it comes, *will do so on the Arabs' timetable, not Israel's.* Unfortunately, all the evidence indicates the Arab world is not about to choose genuine peace with Israel in the foreseeable future. *This lack of control over a painful situation led many Israelis to embrace delusions of control; delusions that the right concessions could not help but win peace from the Arabs.*[10]

And so Israel, sometimes voluntarily, sometimes under pressure from the West — including, sadly, from George W. Bush and the hapless Condoleezza Rice, both of whom, in earlier times, would have known better — continues to give

---

[10] Interview with Dr. Kevin Levin in *FrontPage Magazine.com,* November 25, 2005, http://www.frontpagemag.com/Articles/ReadArticle.asp?ID=20222. (emphases added)

in to Palestinian demands, hoping to keep the "peace process" going, hoping that each new concession will be *the* concession — the one final, definitive act of appeasement that will prompt people who have dedicated their lives to her destruction, who *do not even include Israel on their maps*, to do something — anything — tangible to, however vaguely, give at least a modicum of an indication of a desire, someday, maybe, perhaps, possibly, to make peace. But of course, any clear-thinking person — in other words, anyone not suffering from Oslo Syndrome — can see that nothing Israel does will ever be enough, that each concession will be followed by more demands, for new concessions, until Israel becomes "concessioned out," having given everything she has to give — her security, her sovereignty, her citizens' very lives.

Where is the Israeli leader who understands what Dr. Levin does — that peace will come when, and only when, the Muslim Palestinians are ready. Until they are, Israel can do nothing but see to her own security, and wait. And stop wasting time on useless negotiations.

What's So Precious About Muslims?

Christian Palestinians, on the other hand, I believe, are ready to make *now*. The would sign a peace treaty with Israel today, *if they could*.

The reason they can't, of course, is because they are under the thumb of the Muslim Palestinian majority, powerless to speak — and negotiate — for themselves.

The practical argument for Jewish Palestinians (Israelis) reaching out to those of their Christian Palestinian counterparts living in Judea, Samaria and Gaza and enabling them to determine their own future, *in their own state*, is obvious, and compelling. Just look at the peaceful relations Jewish and Christian (and, yes, Muslim) Palestinians living together, in Israel, enjoy today. Is it not obvious that relations between Israel, as a whole, and a Christian state next door, especially if Israel helps to create that state, would be equally cordial? How could it *not* advantage Israel to have at least one friendly, *Christian* state on her border, among all the Muslim ones?

And the *dis*advantages of a Christian state, living beside Israel, in peace (as, I believe, it most certainly would)? I can't think of any. Can you?

Nor can I think of any *practical* reason why a single, comprehensive peace must be made everywhere, for everyone, at one time. A peace treaty between Israel and the Christian Palestinians today does not preclude Muslim Palestinians from making their own, separate, peace, tomorrow.

I also question—no, I reject—the assumption that there can only be a single "Palestinian state" in all of Judea, Samaria and Gaza. A "Palestinian state" can have only one purpose, which, contrary to the belief of many, is not to make it easier to attack Israel. The idea is to make life better for the people who would live in it—an idea that is absurd for Christian Palestinians, whose lives, I have shown in this book, would be worse, not better, in a Muslim-majority "Palestinian state." Indeed, I would argue that such a state, governed by the same incompetents who are governing it now, would continue, perpetuate and probably accelerate the deterioration in conditions for *Muslim* Palestinians, who, any objective comparison of pre- and post-Arafat Judea, Samaria and Gaza shows, would be far better off under Israeli rule. (For that matter, so would Egyptians, Jordanians, Lebanese and Syrians, but why rub salt into the wound?)

Clearly, for far too many people, a single "Palestinian state" has become an end in itself, a tautology, stripped bare of any consideration of its practical consequences. There must be a Palestinian state because there must be a Palestinian state.

I say, there can be *two* Palestinian states. And even *three*. As will discuss more fully later, the Gaza strip, today, ruled by Hamas, is a virtual separate state. Putting a Christian state in Judea, between the *de facto* separate "states" of "Hamastan" (Gaza) and "Fatahstan" (Samaria) does no practical harm to law-abiding, non-jihadist Muslim and Christian Palestinians. Coexisting within a single state or divided into two or more separate states, neither Muslim Palestinians nor Christian Palestinians would be any more, or any less, economically dependent upon Israel than they are today. They would still, assuming the security wall comes down, be able to commute to jobs in Israel, still able to trade with her.

The only *practical* negative—and only to jihadists—is that jihadists would find it much more difficult, if not impossible, to wage war against Israel. But making war against Israel impossible is what we all should want, isn't it, if the goal is peace?

If Christian Palestinians are willing to negotiate with Jewish Palestinians (Israelis), and vice-versa, why should they be prevented from doing so by Muslim Palestinians? If, as is the present case, Christians are nonviolent, do not, never have and never will threaten Israel, thus making the security wall unnecessary *for Christians*, why should they be denied a way—physical separation in their own state—to tear down the wall between Israelis *and Christian Palestinians*? Why should Christian Palestinians be punished for the violence perpetrated by—and *only* by—Muslim Palestinians?

Nor, incidentally, would taking down the security wall between today Israel and the Christian Palestinians today prevent taking down the wall between Muslim Palestinians tomorrow—*if they adopt the same posture of complete docility and nonviolence as the Christian Palestinians?*

Which raises an important question, a question that is as obvious as the answer, yet no one, apparently, bothers—or dares—to ask:

> *If Christian Palestinians and Muslim Palestinians live in the same area, under the same conditions, and Christian Palestinians are nonviolent, why can Muslim Palestinians not be nonviolent as well?*

Or to put it another way, what is the difference between Christian Palestinians and Muslim Palestinians? The answer, of course, is, another tautology: the Christian Palestinians are Christian; the Muslims are Muslim. In these politically correct times, the international community treads lightly about the issue, few will even entertain it, but the plain fact of the matter is, the Muslim Palestinians would not be attacking Israel if the Muslims were Christians.

But not admitting an obvious truth is not the same as not knowing it. Much of the international community, especially Europe, knows very well that Muslim Palestinians are not engaged in a secular quest for nationhood and self-determination, but a religious war waged by Muslims against Jews. A bold accusation, perhaps, but the repeated condemnations of Israel and calls for her to make concessions *without demanding that Muslim Palestinians end their violence first* proves it, beyond question.

I will go even farther and say that, because so much of the international community does not treat Israel, the only Jewish state, as they would treat any other *democratic, non-terrorist* state that successfully defend itself against genocidal aggressors and require Muslim Palestinians to acknowledge that:

- they have *lost* their *strictly religious* war against Israel;
- as the losers of a war, they are in no position to make demands;
- any talks between Israel and Muslim Palestinians are *not* "negotiations" between "equal adversaries," but between *victor* and *vanquished*;
- if the Muslim Palestinians cannot, or will not, come to terms with Israel, Israel, like the victorious Allies in both World Wars, has the absolute right to *impose her own terms on the losers*

a significant portion of the international *want the Muslim Palestinians to win.*

Now, I am not saying that there are not people who sincerely want peace and believe, however mistakenly, that the path to that peace is to reward Muslim Palestinian intransigence and failure to recognize that *they have lost* by demanding endless concessions from Israel, up to and including a return to the insecure 1949 armistice line, while demanding from Muslim Palestinians, nothing. But it is equally undeniable that there are many people, such as the French diplomat who referred to Israel as "that shitty little country," and the BBC, who hate Israel — and, let's be honest, Jews — and are all but openly colluding with the Muslim Palestinians to achieve for them the victory they could never achieve on the battlefield. To such people, unfortunately, the collateral damage to Christian Palestinians, and, indeed, to ordinary, non-jihadist Muslim Palestinians, is of no concern. I'm reminded of Golda Meir's famous statement, that when the Palestinians love their children more than they hate Jews, there will be peace. Likewise, when the international community's concern for the lives of ordinary Muslim and Christian Palestinians outweighs their prejudice against Israel, and Jews, there will be peace

That I am right is easily proved by looking at two countries that suffered much more devastating defeats, in a much more destructive war: Nazi Germany and Imperial Japan. In World War II, both countries were forced to surrender unconditionally to the victorious Allies, who then proceeded to occupy the two defeated countries; depose their leaders, imprisoning and executing some; dictate their form of government—and even, in the case of Japan, change her religion.[11] All this happened in 1945—for all practical purposes, the same time, ,1948, that Muslim anti-Semites suffered their first of *several* defeats at the hands of Israel. And now, look at Germany, Japan, Judea, Samaria and Gaza today. Germany and Japan are peaceful and prosperous precisely because, for them, the war ended 63 years ago. Indeed, the Germans and Japanese became pacifists. The Muslim Palestinians of Judea, Samaria and Gaza, on the other hand, never laid down their arms and continue to fight, with results that anyone can see: stagnation, poverty and thousands (because they cannot win) of needless Palestinian deaths (and possibly many, many more depending on how long it takes the Muslim Palestinians to acknowledge their defeat).

In 1967, Muslim Palestinians and their allies in the surrounding Arab countries suffered a humiliating defeat in the Six Day War with Israel, but no more humiliating, and not nearly as physically destructive as what Germany and Japan suffered a generation earlier. Imagine, then, that the Americans, Japanese and French allowed the Israelis to do what they allowed themselves to do a generation earlier: occupy the capitals of the states that attacked her, remove the autocracies that ruled them impose new, democratic

---

[11] Until the end of the War, the emperor was considered divine and worshipped as a deity, for whom the Japanese were required to, if called on to do so, sacrifice their lives in return for eternal reward in the afterlife. The divinely-inspired kamikaze pilot of World War II was the precise equivalent of today's jihadist suicide bomber.

governments in their place, including, if necessary, even writing the new governments' constitutions for them? Can there be the slightest doubt that every one of those states would be better off today?

Of course, they would be, and that includes not just Muslims, but Jews and Christians, as well. Which is precisely my point. Christian Palestinians, *do not* need to be convinced to lay down their arms *because they never picked them up in the first place*. Christian Palestinians do not need to be convinced to become pacifists, they *already are* pacifists. Likewise, the Jewish Palestinians (Israelis), who repeatedly target jihadist Muslims, do not target Christian Palestinians and, there can be no doubt, would sign a peace treaty with Christian Palestinians today, if they could—and that's assuming, which I do not, that a treaty is even necessary, since there are current hostilities between Jewish Palestinians (Israelis) and Christian Palestinians and Israel clearly does not consider the latter to be a threat. So why can't they?

> *If Christian Palestinians are willing to make peace with the Israel today, and Israel is willing to make peace with Christian Palestinians, why should they not be able to do so? If Christian Palestinians are ready for peace, why should Muslim Palestinians be allowed to keep them in a perpetual state of war?*

Certainly, there are no *practical* impediments. For example, as I will argue later on, Israel has more than enough military power to:

- retake all of Judea, Samaria and Gaza,
- create a secure Christian enclave in Judea,
- and reroute the portion of the security wall that currently runs north-to-south between Jewish

Palestinians (Israelis) and Christian Palestinians, to run east-to-west, between Judea and Samaria.

Furthermore, as I also will argue, however much certain elements of the international community may protest, once the deed is done, and the improvement in the lives of the Christian Palestinians *and the hundreds of thousands of Christian victims of Muslim and Hindu persecution that immigrate* becomes undeniable, the international community will find it very difficult, and I would argue, impossible, to argue for a return to the old order.

The Moral Case

I just argued the absence of any *practical* reason why the Israel could not or should not negotiate with Christian Palestinians and why those negotiations could not lead to the establishment of a Christian state. Indeed, except for Israel, Egypt, and Iran (formerly called Persia, but the same country), historical states with long and glorious histories, *all* the states in the region are artificial creations carved out of the defeated Ottoman Empire after the World War I. Today's current Judea, Samaria and Gaza are, for all practical purposes, the remaining part of the Ottoman Empire that the Allies "never got to." There, the artificial state — *or states* — are yet to be created, and there is no practical reason why the area cannot be divided into two states, or even three. Indeed, one could argue, with Hamas' takeover of the Gaza Strip, Gaza is now "Hamastan," a *de facto* separate Muslim state. If tiny Gaza can, for all practical purposes, be a separate, sovereign entity, why can't Judea be a separate, sovereign *Christian* entity?

That, in a nutshell, is the practical argument. But the practical argument does double duty as a moral argument, too, for what is the *moral* justification for not allowing Jewish Palestinians (Israelis) and Christian Palestinians from pursuing peace, if both sides are willing? And, given that the

United Nations, in its historic 1947 vote, recognized the Jewish Palestinians' right to self-determination *in their own state;* the international community's subsequent recognition of the Jewish state; its equal recognition of Lebanon, which, as we learned[12], was originally conceived as a Christian state; and the existence of 22 Muslim Middle East state (and calls for a 23rd in Judea, Samaria and Gaza), what is the *moral* justification for denying *Christian* Palestinians *their* equal right to self-determination in *their* own state?

The moral case for a *Christian* state is easily made because it is the same as that was made, successfully — and certified by the international community, in the United Nations, in 1947 — to return the Kingdom of Israel to its original, rightful owners that they might re-establish it as a modern, democratic state. Granted, Israel's rebirth was a return of stolen property, the ending of 2,000 years of foreign occupation, while a Christian state, like the 23rd Muslim state that could have been created in 1947 had the Jordanians and Egyptians not illegally invaded and occupied Judea, Samaria and Gaza (if the UN voted for these invasions, please show me the official record), would be the creation of something new. But then, as I just reminded you, *all* the states, except Israel, Egypt and Iran (Persia) were new creations, too, by powers operating under international (League of Nations, predecessor of the UN) mandate. How, then, can the same UN that supported the partitioning of land between Muslim Palestinians and Christian Palestinians on the one hand, and Jewish Palestinians, on the other, credibly oppose[13] a similar partition of land, in the same area, between Muslim Palestinians and Christian Palestinians? On what *moral* basis does one conclude that the Middle East's Muslims have the

---

[12] See page 32.

[13] I use the term "credibly *opposing*" as opposed to "credibly *voting against*" because I do not envision any vote — indeed, any say at all — by the UN on the matter of establishing a Christian state. The UN-sanctioned British mandate is long gone and with it, the UN's authority. It is strictly a matter between Israel and the Christian Palestinians, to be decided by them alone.

right of self-determination in 22 (and perhaps, one day, 23) states, Jews in one state—but *Christians* in *none?*

The deprivation of rights, the theft and destruction of property, the business boycotts, the physical violence—all the incidents I have cataloged here, and all of which surely would continue in a Muslim-majority state—only strengthen the argument for a Christian state. Indeed, Christian Palestinians suffer much more grievously today than did the Jewish Palestinians, who, unlike today's Christian Palestinians, had a paramilitary self-defense organization, the Palmah, and the heroic aid of patriotic Muslims, such as the Druze and the Bedouins,[14] in 1947.

That Christians will never achieve self-determination in the Middle East *without* their own state, is clear, for as Walid Phares explains:

> The ruling Sunni Muslim and Arabic-speaking regimes of the Middle East disagree on many things, but on one thing they all concur: *non-Arabs ... in their midst must not have political power.* Symbolic of this consensus, the Arab League has *refused to recognize the right of any Christian minority to establish its autonomy,* whether through military means or political dialog.[15]

Thus, it is clear that if Christians are to establish their own, Middle Eastern state, they will need the help of outside powers, chief among whom, I soon will argue, is Israel. But why should Israel support a Christian state on her border? How does she benefit? I answer that question in the next chapter.

---

[14] And who serve, voluntarily, and at higher rates than Jewish Israelis, in the Israeli Defense Forces today.
[15] Walid Phares. (emphases added)

BENEFITS OF A CHRISTIAN STATE

In the preceding chapter, I showed why the international community should support the creation of a Middle Eastern Christian state. In this chapter, I will explain why not just Christians, but Jews and, yes, Muslims, should *welcome* one. But let's begin with Christians, the most obvious beneficiaries of a Christian state.

Benefits to Christians

The greatest benefit Christians would enjoy in their own state is relief from the kinds of discrimination, restrictions, indignities, assaults, and murder Christians inside and outside the Middle East suffer under Muslim and, in India's case, Hindu rule described in this book. In a Christian state:

- Women would not worry about being accosted by roving gangs of "morality police" for failing to cover themselves from head to toe in Islamic garb; they could, without fear, dress for the 21st century, not the seventh. [1]
- A Christian man would not be blinded for life after filing a formal complaint against a Muslim driver who ran over two of his relatives.[2]

---

[1] See page 17.
[2] See page 22.

- Christians would not face arrest for eating or smoking in public during the Muslim's Ramadan holiday.[3]
- The president of a Christian state would not seize monasteries for his and his cronies' personal use.[4]
- The courts of a Christian state would not condone, let alone collude in land theft.[5]

In a nutshell, no Christian-state Muslim would have to fear be treated by Christians the way Muslims treat Christians in Judea, Samaria and Gaza. Nor, I hasten to add, would any non-Christian minorities, including Muslims, need to fear such treatment by the Christian majority. Muslims, I am confident, would be as free in a Christian state as they are, today, in Israel—freer, by far, than they are in any Middle Eastern Muslim state.

Emigration

One of the saddest, and ignored by the international community, results of Oslo and Israel's disastrous decision to allow Arafat and his terrorist gang into Judea, Samaria and Gaza, has been the massive emigration of Christian Palestinians from those areas, a virtual mass-expulsion that was, and is, deliberately abetted by Arafat and the PA. Had Judea been a Christian state in 1993, the year of Arafat's arrival, most if not all of the Christians forced out since then would still be there. Indeed, had the UN had the wisdom to create a Christian state in 1947, at the same time it endorsed Israel's rebirth and return to its original, rightful owners, surely the Christian population of Judea, Samaria and Gaza would be even larger than it was in 1993. Indeed, can we go even farther and speculate that, instead of declining, the

[3] See page 13.
[4] See page 14.
[5] See page 16.

Christian population of a Christian state would have *tripled* since 1948, as it has in Israel?

In any case, it goes without saying that if, say, Judea, were to become a Christian state, the current hemorrhaging of Christians from Judea would stop—and reverse, if not through the return of Christian Palestinians forced out, then through the immigration of even a tiny portion of the world's 2.6 billion Christians, both persecuted and non-persecuted. With a pool of 2.6 *billion* from which to draw, I would be surprised not to see a massive influx of Christians of *all* nationalities and ethnicities, persecuted and non-persecuted, from all over the world. Look at the numbers non-persecuted Jews—free, prosperous, born and raised in democratic countries—who have left friends, family and comfortable lifestyles behind to help Israel reclaim the land after 2,000 years of neglect by foreign occupiers. Is it conceivable that *Christians* would be any less eager to build a *Christian* state? Indeed, as a candidate for Congress in Tennessee told me recently, the problem, for a Christian state, would not be attracting enough Christians to populate it, but accommodating the millions of Christians who would want to come—and incidentally, to whom I would reply: Many Israelis, in 1948, questioned whether their new state could hold more than the 600,000 or so Jews dwelling there at that time. Today, there are 4.5 *million* Jews, plus well over a million non-Jews. New York City, where I live, has a population of 8 million.

Tourism

"Strength in numbers" has a pecuniary meaning, too, for 2.6 billion Christians constitute an enormous financial base on which to build a Christian state. Surely, if Israel's experience is any guide, a Christian state could expect much financial support in the form of direct contributions. But Israel's experience also tells us that, for every Christian who donates emigrates to the Christian state, many, many more would come just to visit—and spend. And remember: There are Jewish shrines in Judea, too, so Jewish tourists to Israel would also want to visit the Christian state, just as Christians visit Israel today. I cannot imagine but that most tourists visiting the Holy Land would want to see *both* states, increasing both states' tourism, prosperity and—so important for the sake of peace—interdependence.

Incidentally, the same would be true for a *Muslim* Palestinian state, when and if Muslim Palestinians come to their senses. I remember my own, 1968, tour of Israel *and* Judea, Samaria and Gaza—the brisk tourist trade I saw in Judea, Samaria and Gaza, pre-Arafat, when Israel still administered these areas and they were peaceful and just beginning to prosper after two decades of Jordanian occupation. Imagine then, a jihadist-free Christian state, with Bethlehem as her capital, and no security wall separating the Christian state from the Jewish one because, with the jihadists walled off from both Jewish Palestinians and Christian Palestinians (or whatever name they choose for themselves, just as the Jewish Palestinians now call themselves Israelis), no wall between Jewish and Christian Palestinians would be necessary. How crowded would the stores, whether owned by Christians or those Muslims as fortunate to be citizens of the Christian state as 1.5 million Muslims are to be Israelis, be? How crowded the hotels? The restaurants? *The churches?*

Protection of Religious Sites

When Muslim jihadists violated the Church of the Nativity in 2002,[6] Christians around the world learned the kind of respect—or disrespect—could expect for their holy sites in a Muslim-majority "Palestinian state." Jews, of course, learned their lesson two years earlier, when "hundreds of Palestinians overran ... Joseph's Tomb ... hours after it was vacated by Israeli troops," and "burned the compound and tore it apart with pickaxes, sledgehammers and their bare hands."[7] Since then, as I described earlier, Christian Palestinians have had to contend with numerous Muslim Palestinian affronts to their own religious sites, including the deliberate building of mosques adjacent to churches, even in Manger Square;[8] the breaching of an ancient church's wall to annex part of its space to an adjacent mosque,[9] and Yasser Arafat's appropriation of a monastery as his personal domicile.[10]

Can there be any doubt that Christian Palestinians would show far more respect for their own shrines than the Muslim Palestinians have? Indeed, can there be any doubt that Christians would extend that same degree of respect to non-Muslim shrines, just as Jews respect the integrity of Christian and Muslim shrines?

Spreading the Word

This next one's a no-brainer. Clearly, Middle Eastern Christians would benefit from being able freely both to hear and to publish the Christian message. In today's Middle East, it is extremely difficult, if not impossible, for Christians to do either. Middle East Christians enjoy virtually nothing in the way of Christian television and radio programming, while being inundated, constantly, with Islamic religious thought.

Christians also are exposed to the most hateful jihadist, anti-Semitic propaganda as well as the latest

---

[7] Joel Greenberg, "Whose Holy Land? At the Shrine; Palestinians Destroy Israeli Site That Was Scene of Many Clashes," *New York Times*, October 8, 2000.
[8] Compare this practice to Egypt's law (see page 48) prohibiting construction of a church within 100 meters of a mosque.
[9] See page 14
[10] See page 14.

pronouncements of Osama bin Laden.[11] One especially notorious example, sufficiently egregious to make newscasts worldwide, was that of Farfur, the infamous Farfur, the "Terror Mouse" of Palestinian children's television. Farfur, a Mickey-Mouse lookalike, would regularly exhort Muslim Palestinian children to sacrifice their lives for Allah in glorious jihad against Jews — that is, until poor Farfur was murdered, on television, *in front of the young children appearing on the show*, by those mean Israelis, when Farfur refused to sell his land to the evil Jews.[12] But if you want your kid to grow up to be a suicide bomber (or become one *before* he grows up), fear not, for almost before one could say "72 virgins" (virgin mice, presumably), Farfur the "Terror Mouse" was quickly replaced by Nahool, the "Jihad Bee," who picked up right where Farfur left off, filling impressionable young minds with such wholesome entertainment as this on-air exchange, in which Nahool asks a young girl, Sabah, who phones into the show, what she wants to be when she grows up;

> **Sabah:** "Journalist."
>
> **Saraai, girl in studio:** "Wow, journalist! Nahool, we need journalists."
>
> **Nahool:** "Why? So that ... they will photograph the Jews when they are killing Farfur and the little children?
>
> **Saraai':** "Yes, Nahool."
>
> **Another young caller:** "We will go on [the path] of Jihad when we grow up."

---

[11] For readers interested in experiencing such messages for themselves, the Middle East Media Research Institute monitors Muslim countries' media and translates them into English, Their Web site, at http://www.memri.org, contains numerous contemporary examples of Middle Eastern Muslim broadcasts, journalism, editorial cartoons, etc.

[12] Farfur's demise can be viewed online at http://www.youtube.com/watch?v =z9IL81QhiR8&NR=1. Other videoclips available by visiting http://www.youtube .com and typing "Farfur" into the search field.

Nahool: "Yes, we are all Jihad warriors."

Saraai': "Allah willing."[13]

Sadly, for young Muslim Palestinian jihadist wannabes, Nahool, the "Jihad Bee," did not last long, either, perishing after the mean Israelis refused to allow him to leave Gaza for medical treatment, and has since been replaced by Assud, the "Jew-eating Rabbit."[14]

Sesame Street, it ain't. Needless to say, Christian media, in a Christian state, would not broadcast such filth.

Education

As pernicious as we've just seen Muslim Palestinian TV is (you don't seriously think *Christian* Palestinians are producing this rot, do you?), what they're taught in the schools is just as bad — so bad that despite what must be a severe financial burden in today's economically depressed Judea, Samaria and Gaza, Christian parents send their children to expensive private schools. As one observer put it, "I have talked to Christian families about what is taught in the schools. From what they say, there is indeed a 'culture of death' that includes glorification of suicide bombers and training to kill Jews and Americans."[15]

In a Christian state, some parents might still choose to send their kids to private schools. But if they did, it would be for the same reason Western parents send their kids to private schools and not to shield their children from the anti-Semitic jihadist crap the Muslim Palestinian education teaches.

A Christian state's public schools would teach a culture of life, not death.

---

[13] Al-Aqsa TV (Hamas), July 20, 2007. Cited by Itamar Marcus and Barbara Cook, "Blood libels on Hamas TV," *Palestinian Media Watch*. Available online at http://pmw.org.il./bulletins_jul2007.htm. Nahool video can be viewed online at http://www.youtube.com/watch?v=tneSE6nJiLw.
[14] Assud video viewable online at http://www.youtube.com/watch?v=Jm8w7 _P8wZ0.
[15] Weiner, 8.

The Muslim Middle East's Greatest Fear

Though they would never publicly admit it, Muslim governments have a very good reason to suppress the Christian message as ruthlessly as they do. The "dirty little secret" many Muslim knows, but few will admit, is that, were Middle Eastern Muslims allowed to hear the Christian message, and to follow their consciences freely, many—no, make that *very* many—would convert. How many? We can get a pretty good idea from the number of Muslims who already *have* converted, in the face of terrible repression, including torture and death. I have described a few in this book[16]; a brief session with your favorite Internet search engine will, I am sure, reveal many more. The televised conversion of former Muslim, Magdi Allam, to Catholicism, on Easter, by the Pope, was a theological shot across the bow that sent shockwaves throughout the Muslim *umma*.

Obviously, a Christian state would disseminate Christian thought and literature to her own citizens. However, *all* Christians, within *and outside* the Christian state, would benefit from the existence of a secure base from which to broadcast peaceful, life-affirming Christian programming to Christians residing not only within her borders, but throughout the Middle East. Is it not high time for the warmongers to have some competition from the peacemongers? At the same time Muslim jihadists are smuggling weapons into, say, Samaria and Gaza, what if there were also Christian pacifists smuggling New Testaments and other Christian literature *in?* Will it not be interesting to see which weapon—the Muslim gun or the Christian Word—ultimately prevails?

And surely, Muslims will not object. If Islam (and, for that matter, Judaism) is strong, Muslims should not fear competition from new ideas. Or for that matter (if I may

---

[16] See entire chapter, "Persecution of Christian Converts," beginning on page 9797.

briefly digress), Jews. What most excites me about the rising tide, worldwide, of Evangelicalism and global Southern Christianity, is Evangelicals' affinity with, and respect for, Christianity's Jewish roots. I would like nothing better than to see the comity between Christians and Jews in America to be duplicated around the world, but especially in the Middle East.

And, though we are talking about benefits to Christians, I cannot resist mentioning that, because some branches of Christianity, such as Evangelicals and global Southern African Christians, identify so closely with Jews, and devote so much of their exegesis to the Old Testament, the dissemination of Christian thought can also, indirectly, be a *de facto* dissemination of Jewish thought. I won't tell if you won't.

But getting back to Christians, what if, in addition to theological programming, there were a "Christian Al Jazeera" broadcasting alongside Al Jazeera, across the Middle East, beaming news, events and opinion from a *Christian* perspective, into every Muslim Middle Eastern country? What if the next televised interfaith debate had a *Christian* moderator?

Think about it.

A Haven for Converts . . .

In this book, I devoted a special chapter just to the treatment of Muslim and Hindu Christian converts. Needless to say, Muslims and Hindus who have converted, or are planning to, would be greatly helped—and saved—by having a Middle Eastern Christian state that, unlike the Christian-majority, but secular, states, that often turn refugees away, would take them in without reservation. Middle Eastern converts would find a nearby Christian state especially advantageous. Theoretically, a Muslim wishing to convert could enter the Christian state on foot, as a tourist or day-laborer and, once safely inside, convert and never go back.

A (Military) Force to Be Reckoned With

Nowhere does the phrase, "strength in numbers," carry more meaning than in the Middle East. 4.5 million Jews, consolidated within their own state are strong. Three times as many Christians, 14 million, dispersed across the Middle East. Why?

The Jews are strong and the Christians are weak because *the Jews have an army and the Christians do not.*

It really is that simple, as graphically demonstrated in Lebanon, where the Muslim terrorist group, Hezbollah, and their puppet-masters, Iran, aided and abetted by Syria, pushes the Christians out of south Lebanon, turns Lebanon into a virtual terrorist state, and the Christians powerless to do anything about it. In earlier times, when there were Christian militias, allied with Israel, patrolling the area, the situation was different. Today, Christian Lebanese find themselves in the same position as their co-religionists in Judea, Samaria and Gaza: pacifists forced to suffer the collateral damage brought down on them by a warmongering majority.

But put these Christians — of Judea, Samaria, Gaza, south Lebanon, Egypt and many other countries — together, like the Israelis, in a sovereign state, *with an army to defend it,* and the result would be a Middle Eastern Switzerland, with a defense force that, like Switzerland's, would exist not to project power abroad, but to make other countries respect her desire to remain neutral, whose citizens would not participate in other states' conflicts, but would take in the wounded and refugees from both sides.

> **A Middle Eastern Christian — and only a Middle Eastern   Christian   state — would   remove**

Christians from the fighting between Jews and Muslims.

The Israel-Christian State Alliance

Of course, in the Muslim-Jewish religious war, one side, Israel's, purpose, to prevent the jihadists from fulfilling their vow to "push the Jews into the sea," is also strictly defensive, Israel and the Christian state would be natural allies, bound by a collective pledge to defend *both* states. That is why it greatly behooves Israel, *for her own sake*, to help establish a Christian state and then work with it to build a strong Christian army not needing Israel's protection, but capable of fighting alongside her.

But I will make that argument later. For now, imagine, a Christian state, with a Christian defense force not just allied with Israel, but *trained and equipped* by the Israel Defense Force, one of the best in the world and certainly the best in the Middle East. The argument becomes even stronger when we realize how many *Christians* serve in the Israeli army. Surely, these Christian Israeli officers would be willing, indeed eager, to help build a *Christian* army to protect *Christians.*

And on the Christian side of the fence, we can easily speculate on the number of Christian veterans of other countries' armies—the British, Australian, French—and of course, the greatest military force in the world (in my humble, admittedly biased, opinion), the U.S. military. The number and quality of military experts eager to help the Christian state develop the means to defend herself—and persecuted Christians around the world—truly would be an embarrassment of riches. And, again, with a pool of 2.6 billion from which to draw, containing literally millions of veterans, recruitment should not be a problem. Adopting Israel's policy of universal, compulsory military service for

Christian state citizens would further ensure a well-manned defense force.

Most important, for a pacifist state, as I would envision the Christian state to be, would be the "deterrent effect." A credible army, even if it is never called upon to fight, would confer an extra degree of legitimacy on the Christian state: There is a major difference between a physically weak "Blanche DuBois state" that "depends on the kindness of strangers" for its security, and one fully capable of defending herself.

Israel

One of the greatest benefits a Christian state could provide to Christians is a restoration of what they had before the Muslim Palestinians launched their insane religious war: access to Israel — Israeli jobs, Israeli trade, Israeli investment, Israeli universities, all the benefits that Israel offers to *all* Palestinians and which all Palestinians could be enjoying today, absent the Muslim Palestinians' self-destructive, anti-Semitic "resistance." Indeed, as I will later show, many non-jihadist Muslim Palestinians having reached the same conclusion, would welcome an end to the "resistance" if for no other reason than to prevent Hamas from taking over Judea and Samaria, but also, generally, to restore the pre-Arafat security, growing prosperity and, above all, *a burgeoning middle class.*

For that — the elimination of the Muslim Palestinian and Christian Palestinian middle class — certainly was one of the jihadists' goals and it is clear that they were quite successful in achieving it. Indeed, and unfortunately for Palestinians, both Christian and Muslim, it was the jihadists' *only* success. The plan to cripple Israel economically by cutting off Israel's access to Palestinian labor (those jobs have long ago been filled by Thais and Chinese) has failed miserably; Israel's economy and her currency, the shekel, has never been stronger. The security wall has been extraordinarily effective in preventing the suicide bombings intended to make daily life, for the average Israeli, intolerable. In other words, in trying to hurt Israel, the Muslim Palestinians have succeeded only in hurting themselves — and, of course, the Christian Palestinian minority dwelling among them.

Well, that was the Muslim Palestinians' decision. *But was it the Christians?* Might Christian Palestinians, perhaps, possibly, just maybe prefer jobs to jihad? If they would rather work and trade than fight, *should they not be allowed to?*

Of course, in their own state, Christian Palestinians could just as well choose to fight as not to, but if they did, at least, *it would be their decision.* And if Christian Palestinians choose not to fight, as is the case today, they have imposed upon them the price for the Muslim Palestinians' opposite decision?

> **Would it not greatly advantage Christian Palestinians to be free, in their own state, to choose their own course — whether to fight Israel or make peace with her?**

Benefits to Jews

The late Israeli diplomat, Abba Eban, famously chided the Muslim Palestinians for "never missing an opportunity to miss an opportunity," but he could just as well have been talking about Israel. Time and again, throughout Israel's turbulent history, as Islamic Arabia has become increasingly radicalized, as Hezbollah has entrenched itself in Lebanon, as the threats of Hamas, the Al Aqsa Martyrs Brigades, Islamic Jihad and others have festered in Judea, Samaria and Gaza, Israel has squandered repeated opportunities to enhance her own security by helping the Middle East's Christians to enhance theirs. Nowhere was this failure to act boldly in her own interest more dramatically demonstrated than in the place where Israel had a golden opportunity to create a secure Christian enclave on her border—one that would serve both as a sanctuary for Christians and as a buffer between Israel and her Muslim enemies—and, in a stunning strategic blunder and lack of vision, thrown it away.

Lebanon.

In June 1982, after repeated provocations from the PLO operating out of southern Lebanon, Israel invaded and set up a "security zone" along Lebanon's southern border. At the same time, she allied herself with the Lebanese Christians and the Christian Phalangist militias, who had by that time established a *Petit Liban*—a Christian enclave that included southern Lebanon, plus eastern Beirut, most of Mount Lebanon and parts of the Beka'a Valley. But as time passed, internal policy divisions among the Christians, combined with external attacks by an alliance of the PLO, other jihadists and the Syrians, to reduce both the areas Christians controlled and the number of Christians living in them. One-by-one, Christian villages were "attacked, razed and ethnically cleansed."[17]

At the same time, Hezbollah began a guerilla offensive against Israel, whose primary effect, over a period of years, was to bring to power, in Israel, a left-wing administration whose first instinct, like that of most left-wing administrations faced with a determined aggressor (as the American left wing wants to flee from Iraq today), was to cut and run. And cut and run, they did, in 2000, when the Israelis abandoned her security zone—and, tragically, the Christians living there.[18]

What Israel *should* have done was, maintain the foundation she established with her security zone, *strengthened* it, and *built upon it*. How? By facilitating the

---

[17] Walid Phares, "Are Christian Enclaves the Solution?"
[18] A small percentage of Christians were allowed to enter Israel.

return to southern Lebanon of as many as possible of the Christians that Muslims and their Syrian patrons had forced out, *plus additional Christians*, from all over the Middle East and, indeed, from the world beyond. Israel's position in Lebanon became untenable for three reasons:

- The Israelis decided, early on, against going all-out, for a decisive victory, opting instead for the kind of holding-action that could not continue indefinitely;
- The Israelis were an outside, occupying force, with no roots in, or attachment to, Lebanon; and, most significant,
- The Christian population, who *did* live there, *did* have their roots there, *were* willing to put their lives on the line to defend it, were too few in number relative to the Muslims.

Simply put, the Christian Lebanese lost (and, absent outside help, probably would in second civil war) because they were (and are) outnumbered.

So imagine this alternative scenario: Imagine that, instead, Israel had, in partnership with the Christians, *declared Lebanon the site of a future Christian state*. Call it, for argument's sake, the state of South Lebanon. Imagine that Israel had spent her time in southern Lebanon helping the Christians (supplemented, I am sure, with substantial aid, both financial and logistical, from the world's 2.6 *billion* Christians) to bring in, say, a couple of million Christians, maybe more. Imagine that, from these millions of Christians, Israel had equipped and trained an effective Christian army. What would have happened?

This is what would have happened.   In 2000, or maybe only two or three years later, Israel could have left, just as she did anyway, *but with a Christian state, instead of Hezbollah, on her border*. And the Christians, for their part, would be safe, *in their own state*, with a Christian army to defend them and a powerful ally, Israel, directly to the south.

This possibility — let's call it "the obvious" — that so eluded Israel's feckless leadership, was as plain as day to a Christian Lebanese soldier, who, under the pseudonym, "N10452," wrote the following in an Internet blog, *The Ouwet Front: Personal Views and Opinions of Lebanese Forces Members*:

> [At the time of the 1982 Lebanon War, then-Israeli General Ariel] Sharon's offer was to ally with Lebanese President Bashir [Gemayel] and support the Christians . . . in Lebanon, *and even had in mind dividing Lebanon, giving the Christians the biggest part and keeping them in full control.*
>
> The Advantages for the Christians were immense: political and military support from Israel and therefore from Americans, a vital alliance with a highly developed country like Israel having an impressive industrial sector. Added to that, the Lebanese lobby would be able to grow stronger working with the most powerful lobby in the world, the Jewish lobby.
>
> *In sum, Christians [would have been] safe and prosperous on all levels,* but [would] have [had] to sacrifice their Arab relations, and their country and [would] be influenced by Israeli's political decisions since [the Christians would be] allying to a much stronger force.
>
> This package was all in Bashir's hands, but he was a leader and a fighter and a president [who] strongly believed in Lebanon and in its people and could not accept allying with another country against his own people.

However, after the Taef agreement[19] and the Muslim political parties' siding with [the] Syrians against Christians, and nowadays with the Shiites taking us into a regional war for a cause we never believed in, we feel that our freedom and equal representation are highly threatened more than ever.

My question is: *[Would it not have been] wise for Sheikh Bashir Gemayel to [have] take[n] this deal and guaranteed the Christians' freedom and sovereignty, knowing that Muslims groups betrayed us for 15 years by obeying the Syrians and persecuting us and weakening us on every possible occasion?*

There is no doubt Bash took a very courageous and, I [believe,] historical decision back then, but looking at what's been happening lately and in the past 15 years, *I don't see why accepting such an alliance would have been the wrong and unpatriotic thing to do.*[20]

Can no one in the current Israeli government see what this Christian Lebanese soldier sees so clearly? After all, an earlier generation of Israeli leaders did, as Walid Phares notes:

Itself a Jewish enclave in a predominantly Muslim region, *Israel at first encouraged the idea of a mosaic of mini-states that would undermine Arab hegemony over non-Arabs.* Well before the establishment of the state, Jewish Agency representatives contacted Maronites, Kurds, and

[19] See page36.
[20] N10452, "Bashir Gemayel & the 1982 Israeli Invasion, *The Ouwet Front: Personal Views and Opinions of Lebanese Forces Members*, August 10, 2006, http://www.ouwet.com/n10452/personal-opinions/bashir-gemayel-the-1982-israeli-invasion. (charmingly fractured English in the original; emphases added)

other minority groups in the Levant. During the first Sudan civil war, Israeli assistance was evident among the southern guerilla forces. In northern Iraq, Israeli intelligence agents supported the Kurds.

But it was in Lebanon that the Jewish state played the card of a Christian enclave to the fullest. In the 1950s, Prime Minister David Ben Gurion actively looked at the possibility of cooperation with a smaller Christian Lebanon, allied to Israel.[21]

The kidnapping of three Israeli soldiers by Hezbollah and the 2006 Lebanon war constitute the latest, but surely not the last, price to be paid by Israel for the failure of Ben Gurion's successors to pick up where he left off. Now the hour is late, but perhaps not too late. With Hezbollah rearming, and with ever more sophisticated weapons, we can confidently predict another war. Needless to say (and as I am confident will be the case if, as I predict, Netanyahu is elected), the Israelis will go in, in force this time, and, this time, finish the job that the hapless Olmert barely began. If they do, Israel should learn from her past mistakes and, this time, ally with Lebanon's Christians to *create a southern Lebanese Christian state—and* help millions of additional Christians to immigrate to the new state, *and* build a credible Christian army. Oh, and make sure the Christian army's area of operation contains a nice chunk of the Lebanese-Syrian border so that if Syria ever decides to do something stupid, she will face attack from two sides.

Do these things and Israel need never worry about being attacked from the north, again.

---

[21] Walid Phares, "Are Christian Enclaves the Solution?". (emphases added)

Golan Heights

Okay, now, this one might seem a stretch, but could the same strategy that would create Christian states in Judea/Samaria/Gaza and southern Lebanon, create at least a Christian enclave, and possibly a Christian state, in the Golan Heights? In one sense, it could actually be easier because Israel currently occupies and fully controls the Heights. She could, if she had the will to do so, implement the strategy I just outlined, *today*. Nothing stops her, today, from admitting an unlimited number of Christians into the area, soliciting help from the world's 2.6 *billion* Christians to finance the venture, and creating from this pool of immigrants, a Christian army capable of defending the heights—which, in fact, might not even be necessary. The Golan's Christian army probably would need only to serve as a "hair trigger" to sound the alarm of a Syrian attack and hold the Syrians off long enough for the Israelis to send reinforcements which, given Israel's proximity to the area, should arrive quickly.

Were the Israelis to do this, we can anticipate a cry of outrage from the international community, but then the international community is always crying about something, isn't it? But just to be sure, the Israelis should endeavor to ensure that the new immigrants contain large numbers of Christians from areas where Christians are most persecuted (which, morally, Israel would want to do, anyway). Then let the international community shame themselves by publicly demanding that Israel deport, say, Christian Sudanese refugees and send them "back where they came from" to be robbed, raped and butchered by the Janjaweed.

But the real beauty of this strategy is, with the Christians officially in control of the Heights (but with full access by Israeli civilians and probably her military, too), the Israelis would be "out of the loop," so to speak, diplomatically, regarding the Golan Heights. If Syria wants to talk to Israel about regaining the Heights, Israel can say, "Golan belongs to the Christians now. You'll have to talk to them."

Neat, huh?

Sheba Farms

Same idea. Take Israel out of the loop. Give Sheba Farms to the Christians.

In Case You Didn't Notice, You're Surrounded

The bad news is, Israel is a tiny country, outnumbered and surrounded by non-Jews. The good news is ... well, actually, there is no good news. The best Israel can hope for is to be able to choose which non-Jews surround her.

The choice is between being surrounded by people who talk like this:

- "We will make the Jews drip tears of blood. We will never find comfort until we shed the blood of sons of monkeys and pigs."[22]
- "[T]here is no solution for the Palestinian question except through Jihad."[23]

Or like this:

- "We don't participate in resistance."[24]
- "One day there will be peace [in Bethlehem] because this is the city of peace and the birthplace of Jesus."[25]
- "I cannot, because of my personal faith, use violence."[26]

For a people who can boast of having won 156 Nobel Prizes (with more to come, I sure), this should be the mother

---

[22] "Iran and Gaza," *The Jerusalem Post*, May 23, 2007.
[23] "Introduction to Palestine."
[24] Chris McGreal, "Homes razed in mob fury at couple's 'affair,'" *The Guardian* (London), September 5, 2005.
[25] Khaled Abu Toameh, "Away from the manger—a Christian-Muslim divide."
[26] Stephen Farrell and Rana Sabbagh Gargour, "All my staff at the church have been killed—they disappeared," *The Times* (London), December 23, 2006.

of all no-brainers. If you're an Israeli, you want Christians, as many as you can get, sharing your borders.

Including Christians who hate you.

The Dhimmis

As strongly as I sympathize with the Christian Palestinians, as strongly as I argue that they deserve their own state, I do not, nor should Israel, turn a blind eye to the virulent anti-Semitism of *some* Christian Palestinians, who hate Israel and Jews as much as, if not more than, do jihadist Muslims. It is a hatred, harbored and natured over many centuries, so deep as to transcend any compassion for the suffering of their fellow Christian Palestinians. Rather than resisting the Muslim Palestinians who directly persecute them—the land-thefts, the forced marriages, the church burnings, the assaults, the rapes, the murders—rather than utter a word of protest against the jihadists who *deliberately* use Christian neighborhoods as sniping posts, rocket-launching sites, staging-grounds for attacks on Israel, and as sanctuaries afterwards so as to draw Israeli retaliation into the neighborhoods of peaceful Christians and away from their fellow Muslim, these dhimmi Christians *collaborate* with them.

Basically, the Christian *dhimmi* is Middle East's "house negro"; however, in the interest of propriety, and because most oppressed Christians chafe under their oppression, resist it whenever possible and above all, are not anti-Semitic, I will refer to these collaborationist Christian minority as precisely that: *collaborationist dhimmis*.

Unlike more enlightened Christians of the modern era, who believe, as Disraeli famously said, that while Christianity "completes" Judaism, it is also incomprehensible without it, or Pastor John Hagee, who said, "Truth is not what I say it is. Truth is not what you think it is. Truth is what the Torah says it is,"[27] collaborationist dhimmis believe in the ancient, discredited doctrine of "supersession," the idea that Christianity made Judaism irrelevant and replaces it entirely. Supersessionist Christians believe that, when the Jews refused to leave the "old" faith for the "new," God cursed them, cast then out of their land and condemned them to "wander" the earth, a stateless people, forever.

Muslims hold the same supersessionist beliefs as dhimmi Christians, which, for these Christians, would be just fine if that were as far as it went (and which, as we shall see presently, is one reason they collaborate so readily with Muslims against Jews). But unfortunately for Christians, what Muslims believe about Judaism, *they also believe about Christianity*—that is, that Islam replaces *both* religions, Judaism *and* Christianity. Thus, pious Muslims hold Christians and Jews in the same low regard. To a seventh century Christian, as bad as it might have been to be conquered and subjugated by Muslims, to be considered, and treated, no better than Jews—to be put on the level of the people to whom they had always felt, always been able to act, superior—was an intolerable humiliation, as Bat Ye'or explains:

> On the doctrinal plane, there is a convergence and fusion between the Christian doctrine that alleges a divine condemnation of the Jews to exile and degradation and the Muslim doctrine that retains the divine condemnation of the Jews to humiliation *but applies it also to Christians*. For Jews, the Islamic position represented an improvement compared to Christian theology, which isolated them from the rest of humanity

---

[27] John Hagee, *United for Israel*, speech delivered to AIPAC Policy Conference, March 11, 2007. (emphases mine)

in a unique, demonized category. For the Christians, to be placed on the same level as the people who aroused their hate-filled contempt was severely felt by them as a further deliberate humiliation imposed on them by Islam. [28]

Unable to raise themselves, in Muslim eyes, to the Muslims' level, the ancestors of the collaborationist dhimmis settled for the next best thing: diminishing, in *their* eye, the Jews. This they did by collaborating with their new Muslim masters in exchange for being allowed to continue, under Muslim rule, the same persecution of the Jews that the Christians had practiced before. If they could not be equal to Muslims, at least they could remain superior to Jews:

> Only a few years before the Arab conquest, . . . the Emperor Heraclius decreed the first massacre of Jews in the Byzantine Empire. It was this same patriarch who later implored the Muslim conquerors to retain . . . the de-Judaism of Jerusalem. Thus, it was through local Christian channels that this policy was transmitted to Islam. Conscious of being the guardians of this doctrine, the churches in the Holy Land heaped humiliation and suffering on Palestinian Jewry and upon the few allowed back in Jerusalem by the Muslim authority.[29]

Thus, without unduly diminishing Muslims' own hostility to the Jews, or excusing their treatment of them, it is nevertheless fair to say that Muslim apologists, such as Bernard Lewis, have a legitimate point when they claim that rather than assigning all the blame for the persecution of

---

[28] Bat Ye'or, "Israel, Christianity, and Islam: The Challenge of the Future," *Midstream*, February/March 2001, http://www.dhimmitude.org/archive/Israel.Christianity.and.Islam.pdf.f
[29] Ibid. (emphases added)

Jews under Islam, early Christians also played a role in determining how anti-Semitism was expressed.

Middle Eastern Christian hostility toward the Jews continued unabated, through the centuries, entrenching itself so deeply in the hearts of dhimmi Christians that as recently as the second Vatican council ("Vatican II") (1963-1965), where the Catholic Church attempted a reconciliation with the Jews, it was "Eastern Arab dhimmi Churches" who stood strongly opposed. And then they went farther, laying the foundation for the present-day tactic of delinking anti-Semitism from anti-Zionism, as if there were any practical difference between the two:

> Despite the efforts of religious and lay Christians who felt close to Judaism, the results of Vatican II marked the success of the anti-Semitic majority in the Catholic church. They maintained a policy of delegitimizing and demonizing the State of Israel, and supported its replacement by a State of Palestine. In other words, the principle of "wandering" remained a decisive goal [and] the condemnation of anti-Semitism was not accompanied by a total rehabilitation of the Jews. This ambiguity allowed Christians to pity the misfortunes of the Jews, allegedly brought about by their own malevolent natures [while reconciling] compassion for Jews with the most virulent hostility towards Israelis. *The transfer of the malevolent nature of the Jews to the State of Israel was steadily sustained by a tireless activism from the Palestinian church leaders allied to the PLO.*

*   *   *

This whole process of demonizing the State of Israel was conceived of, elaborated upon, and transmitted to Europe by these Palestinian dhimmi Arab churches.[30]

America's Christians, happily, were not so easily duped. Indeed no less a religious personage than Martin Luther King, Jr., was unequivocal in stating: "When people criticize Zionists, they mean Jews."[31]

In the 40 years since Vatican II, collaborationist dhimmi Christian Palestinians have made much progress— unfortunately, in the wrong direction. Whereas, in times past, the collaborationist dhimmis merely denied their history under Muslim domination, they now set about *rewriting* it, transforming the historical fact of centuries of humiliating subjugation, into a mythical "golden age" when, as the dhimmis now tell it, Muslims and Christians lived side by side as equals, their relations pleasant and peaceful, where the historical realities of, say, Moorish Spain, where "female Christian slaves taken in continuous border raids filled the Andalusia harems, and the Muslim state's power was based on armed forces made up of thousands of Islamized Christian male slaves," never happened.[32]

To which, the average Jewish Palestinian/Israeli might ask, "So what?" If a dhimmi Christians—and only a minority of them, at that—want to jack up their self-esteem by making up a fantasy Christian history in which Muslims and Christians were equal, why should Jews care?

---

[30] Ibid. (emphases added)

[31] Seymour Martin Lipset, "The Socialism of Fools: The Left, the Jews and Israel," *Encounter*, December 1969. This quote, taken from an appearance by Dr. King at Harvard shortly before his death in 1968, was personally heard by Lipset: "Shortly before he was assassinated, Martin Luther King, Jr., was in Boston on a fund-raising mission, and I had the good fortune to attend a dinner which was given for him in Cambridge... One of the young men present happened to make some remark against the Zionists. Dr. King snapped at him and said, 'Don't talk like that! When people criticize Zionists, they mean Jews. You're talking anti-Semitism!'" Then-civil rights activist, later U.S. Representative John Lewis, who personally knew King, confirmed the quote in an op-ed that appeared in the January 21, 2002 *San Francisco Chronicle*. This statement, confirmed by two sources, is not to be confused with the almost certainly fraudulent (it does not appear in the cited source and the writing style apparently is not of King's) "Letter to an Anti-Zionist Friend."

[32] Bat Ye'or, "Israel, Christianity, and Islam: The Challenge of the Future."

They should care because that particular fantasy comes at a price—to Jews. Assuming, for argument's sake, that the collaborationist dhimmis' "golden age" really existed, then we must ask the obviously question: Why, *today*, is Christian equality with Muslims virtually non-existent in the Muslim world?

The answer, collaborationist dhimmis claim, is that the "golden age" between Christians and Muslims ended *because the Jews ruined it.*

Which, even if that were all there were to it, would be bad enough. But there's more and this "more" has important implications *today*, because the collaborationist dhimmis also believe that their mythical "multicultural paradise" "would be reborn *if only a democratic Arab Palestine were to replace Israel.*"[33] If only Israel could disappear, Christians and Muslims would get along fine. For example, take a look at this statement from Sabeel, the quintessential organization of collaborationist dhimmi Christian Palestinian butt—kissers, in its hilariously misnamed "Principles for a Just Peace in Palestine-Israel."

Note how Sabeel's initially seems to call for the standard "two-state solution." But, as should not surprise us, given the Principles' use of the phrase "Palestine-Israel" in place of "Palestine *and* Israel," the statement quickly veers off in a new direction, calling for a *single* state into which Israel would disappear—and in which, I am sure, though the statement does not explicitly say so, Jews would be a minority:

> Our vision involves two sovereign states, Palestine and Israel, *who will enter into a confederation or even a federation*, possibly with other neighboring countries and where *Jerusalem becomes the federal capital*. Indeed, the ideal and

---

[33] Ibid. (emphasis added)

best solution has always been to envisage ultimately *a bi-national state* in Palestine-Israel where people are free and equal, living under a constitutional democracy that protects and guarantees all their rights, responsibilities, and duties without racism or discrimination. *One state for two nations and three religions.*[34]

The irony, of course, apparent to everyone but the radical left, anti-Semites and many Europeans (or am I being redundant), is that the Sabeel folks live right next door to an *existing* state, the only one in the Middle East in fact, where people *already* are "free and equal, living under a constitutional democracy that protects and guarantees all their rights, responsibilities, and duties without racism or discrimination": Israel.[35]

As we've just seen, rewriting the history of Muslim-Christian relations under Islamic governance eliminated one source of humiliation for the collaborationist dhimmi

---

[34] *Principles for Just Peace in Palestine-Israel*, Sabeel. Viewable online at http://www .sabeel.org/old/justice.

[35] Which is not to say that there is no discrimination in Israel as there is in any other country. It is to say that in Israel, as in any other enlightened democratic country, victims of discrimination have access to the courts, who do not hesitate to rule in the plaintiff's favor, even if the discriminator is the government. Some examples, from the New Israel Fund Web site (http://www.nif.org): "Israeli Employers in the West Bank Ordered to Give Palestinians Full Employment Rights (October 15,2007) ("Israel's Supreme Court has ruled that relations between Israeli employers and Palestinian employees in the West Bank are subject to Israel's labor laws.... [T]he nine judge panel unanimously accepted the claim ... that the two Palestinian employees were entitled to basic social benefits enshrined in Israel labor laws, such as the minimum wage and severance pay); "More Funds for Israeli Arab School" (March 7, 2007) ("Schools in Israel's Arab sector will receive much larger budgets ... following last year's successful petition ... against the government's priority zone status which has been granted to 500 Jewish communities and only four Arab locations. The Court ruled that the policy discriminated against the Arab minority in education, welfare, housing and employment by offering incentives to the almost exclusively Jewish regions included in the program.") "Supreme Court Orders Jewish Village to Allocate Land to Arab Couple" (November 6, 2007) ("Israel's Supreme Court has ordered the village of Rakefet, located in Northern Israel, to allocate land for housing to a young Arab couple.... The ruling comes ahead of a final verdict by the Supreme Court challenging the existence of regional selection committees, which determine whether applicants are 'suitable residents' for the country's rural Jewish villages." The case is also notable in the petition's "claim that the selection committees filter applications form a range of *other minority groups*, including *Mizrachi Jews*, single parents and the lesbian and gay community." (emphases added") In other words, though Arabs are sometimes discriminated against the are not *singled* out for discrimination; others, including Jews, have had the same experience as have Muslims.); "NIF Campaign Against Humiliating Security Checks at Ben Gurion Airport Achieves Results" (March 7, 2007) ("Last week the government announced a commitment to address the often security personnel when flying in and out of Israel."); "Café Cited for Coexistence Efforts" (December 18, 2007) ("Israel is honoring a Jaffa café for fostering Jewish-Arab ties. Since its launch in 2003, the Yaffa Café has been a popular venue for the mixed-race district, offering with its food a selection of books in Hebrew and Arabic about politics and culture. The café was selected from among 30 candidates for the Yisraela Goldblum Prize, which is awarded for initiatives that promote Jewish-Arab coexistence in Israel.

Christians—that of being reduced to the status of Jews. But that still left one more embarrassment unassuaged (and let me be clear, I mean embarrassment to *dhimmi Christians* and perhaps *some* other Christian denominations, I must emphasize, but *not* others, such as, obviously, American Evangelicals). The "embarrassment" is Christianity's obvious and undeniable roots in, and debt to, Judaism. Unlike Disraeli and John Hagee, whom I quoted earlier[36], and many others, who frankly, even proudly, acknowledge Christianity's debt to Judaism because, to state the matter plainly, they are not anti-Semitic. On the other hand, as Bat Ye'or explains, the "filial relationship between Judaism and Christianity is unacceptable and scandalous for Christian Arabs steeped in anti-Judaism."

> Before the creation of the State [of Israel], the Old Testament was considered to be an essential part of Christian Scripture, pointing and witnessing to Jesus. Since the creation of the State, some Jewish and Christian interpreters have read the Old Testament largely as a Zionist text to such an extent that it has become almost repugnant to Palestinian Christians […] The fundamental question of many Christians, whether uttered or not, is: *How can the Old Testament be the Word of God in light of the Palestinian Christians' experience with its use to support Zionism?* [37]

To remove this stain, the undeniable link between Christianity and Judaism, collaborationist dhimmi Christian Palestinians created a new, fantasy theology, "Palestinian Liberation Theology" that transforms Jesus—and Mary, and Joseph, and the

---

[36] See page 147.
[37] Bat Ye'or, "Israel, Christianity, and Islam: The Challenge of the Future."

apostles—from the Galilean Jews that they were, into Palestinian Arabs.[38]

As their mythical "golden age" of Christian-Muslim relations in medieval times, Bat Ye'or writes:

> This travesty would seem childish," if it did not actually express an implicit desire to expel Judaism totally from Christianity and to usurp its heritage through Muslim-Christian Palestinianism. The de-Judaization of Christianity proceeds from a self-destructive dynamic and an impossibility to reconcile the hatred for Jews with the Jewish origin of Christianity. *This hatred is particularly virulent in the historic Palestinian paganized churches – in the Land of Israel itself.*[39]

Christian Dhimmis, the Christian State and Israel

Given the presence of such virulently anti-Semitic Christians in Judea and their certain inclusion in a Christian state, Israelis can justifiably ask themselves, "Do we really want to give these guys their own state?" Yes, you do, for two reasons. First, collaborationist dhimmis are no more than a minority, one that is widely despised by the majority of Christian Palestinians, as Justus Reid Weiner points out:

> There [is] a "180 degree difference" between the public statements coming out of the mainstream Christian leadership in the Holy Land—who "sing the [Palestinian Authority's] tune" and blame Israel for all the Christian Arabs' ills— and people's experience on the ground.[40]

In fact, as we will see later, many *Muslim* Palestinians blame their fellow Muslims and not Israel, for their situation. But I digress. My point is, however much collaborationist Christian

---

[38] Naim Stifan Ateek (1989). *Justice, and Only Justice: A Palestinian Theology of Liberation.* Maryknoll: Orbis Books, 77-78.
[39] Bat Ye'or, "Israel, Christianity, and Islam: The Challenge of the Future." (emphasis added)
[40] Etgar Levkovits.

dhimmis' might despise Jews and Judaism in general and Israel in particular, their *practical* influence, because of their small numbers, on a Christian-state's policies toward Israel would be minimal today—and this is before their relative numbers are even further diminished by the expected influx of millions of new immigrants from the Christian diaspora..

More important is the obvious fact that collaborationist dhimmi Christian Palestinians, unlike Muslim jihadist Palestinians, express whatever hatred they may harbor toward Israel, *nonviolently*. Israelis, therefore, should welcome every opportunity to empower—and line Israel's border with—nonviolent Christians in place of violent jihadist Muslims.

And if I may add a message to dhimmi collaborationist Christian Palestinians: Currently, your thinking is informed by the belief that the only alternatives available to you are life under Jewish, or under Muslim, rule. But in this book, if you will listen, and act, I offer you a third: ruling *yourselves*, beholden to *no one*, in *your own state*.

Surely, you can "collaborate"—even with Jews—to create *that*.

Benefits to Muslims

With the obvious exception of Israel, the Middle Eastern Muslims who would benefit the most, by far, from a Christian state are those Muslims who would be fortunate enough to live in it. Like Muslim Israelis, Muslim Christian-staters would enjoy as much freedom as their Israeli coreligionists and more, much more, than in any Muslim Middle Eastern state.

Opportunity Cost

In economics, "opportunity cost" is the price one pays for economic behavior over another. For example, if I decide (as I so often do) to spend $500 on wine, women and song instead of putting it in an interest-bearing savings account, opportunity cost is the interest I would have earned had I banked, instead of spent, the cash.

In Judea, Samaria and Gaza, opportunity cost is the peace, security and higher standard of living Muslim and Palestinians could be enjoying this very minute, were those areas not infested with jihadists hell-bent on destroying Israel. For example, imagine that all those Muslim Palestinian tool-and-die shops manufacturing Qassam rockets were, instead, filling orders for parts from Israeli manufacturers.

Just how big is this lost opportunity cost? We can get an idea by comparing the economic stagnation we see in Judea, Samaria and Gaza today, to the vibrant economic growth they enjoyed under the Israelis, when Judeans, Samarians and Gazans had access to Israeli trade, investment and jobs. During that time, as Efraim Karsh reports,

> the West Bank and Gaza constituted the fourth fastest-growing economy in the world — ahead of such "wonders" as Singapore, Hong Kong, and Korea, and substantially ahead of Israel itself . . . with per-capita GNP expanding tenfold between 1968 and 1991 from $165 to $1,715 (compared with Jordan's $1,050, Egypt's $600, Turkey's $1,630, and Tunisia's $1,440). By 1999, Palestinian per-capita income was nearly double Syria's, more than four times Yemen's, and 10 percent higher than Jordan's (one of the better-off Arab states). Only the oil-rich Gulf states and Lebanon were more affluent.[41]

---

[41] Efraim Karsh, *What Occupation?*, Commentary (July/August 2002); available by subscription only, on the Commentary Web site, but available without subscription here: http://www.palestinefacts.org/what_ occupation.html.

When Israel—and peace—reigned in her former provinces and Gaza, Palestinians enjoyed:

- Access to, and trade with, Israel, by far the strongest economy in the Middle East;
- Education in Israel's world-class universities, and
- Collaboration with arguably the most, knowledgeable and experienced experts in desert agriculture.

Today, of course, all of that, along with the Palestinian standard of living, is gone and not for the first time. Time and again during the years since the reestablishment of Israel in 1948, Muslim Palestinians, aided and abetted by their enablers in the international community, seized the opportunity, if you will, to prove the truth of Abba Eban's observation that they "never miss the opportunity to miss an opportunity." Only when Muslim Palestinians give up their insane "resistance" and change their self-defeating, self-destructive (and destructive to Christian Palestinians) behavior, will they begin to climb out of the hole they have dug themselves into. Jonathan Schanzer put it well when he wrote:

> [O]ne lesson is glaringly obvious. For the Palestinians to end their misery, they must articulate a forward-looking vision of a Palestinian state built upon the creation of a Palestinian civil society, rather than the destruction of Israel and obsession with mistakes of the past. *Only when Palestinians abandon their resort to uprisings will it be possible to establish a viable Palestinian state, living in peace alongside Israel.*[42]

---

[42] Ibid. (emphasis added)

But that is a decision only the Palestinian Muslims can make. We are all on their timetable; it is a symptom of Oslo Syndrome[43] to think otherwise. Either the jihadist minority changes their attitude or the sensible majority replaces them with new, enlightened leaders. Having a Christian state, living in peace and prosperity beside Israel as an example of the peace, prosperity and security Muslim Palestinians could be enjoying if they, too, made peace with Israel, would make sensible Muslim Palestinians' job much easier.

Muslims for Israel – and for a Christian State, Too?

And they—moderate, modern sensible Muslim Palestinians—do exist, and in larger numbers than some, in this post-9/11 world, might think. We just don't hear much from them, nor are we likely to anytime soon in places like Judea, Samaria and Gaza, where jihadists run the show and any Muslim Palestinian who got up on a soapbox and called for peace with Israel and an end to the "resistance" certainly would be branded a "collaborator" and shot on sight. But other moderate Muslims, living in the West, beyond the range of jihadist reprisals,[44] *are* speaking out, saying what, as we will see presently, many Judean, Samarian and Gazan Muslims would say themselves, but cannot without risking their lives. A good example is an organization, Arabs for Israel, that proudly declares, among other things, on its Web site:

- We can support Israel and still support the Palestinian people. Supporting one does not cancel support for the other.
- We can support the State of Israel and the Jewish religion and still treasure our Arab and Islamic culture.

---

[43] See page 113.
[44] Or are they? Hirsi Ali, probably the most well known Muslim apostate, required 24-hour protection despite living in the supposedly enlightened Netherlands. Since converting to Catholicism—and even before—Magdi Allam has received death threats as has Wafa Sultan, who publicly criticized Islam on Al Jazeera.

- The existence of the State of Israel is a fact that we accept.
- Israel is a legitimate state that is not a threat but an asset in the Middle East.
- Every major World religion has a center of gravity. Islam has Mecca, and Judaism certainly deserves its presence in Israel and Jerusalem.
- It will benefit Arabs to end the boycott of Israel.
- It will be better for Arabs when the Arab media ends the incitement and misinformation that result in Arab street rage and violence.
- We seek dialogue with Israel. We invite you to join us on a path of love.[45]

Needless to say, the live a Muslim Palestinian who invited his fellow Muslim Palestinians to "join him in a path of love" of Israel would not be worth a plugged shekel.

And the love doesn't stop there. Arabs for Israel also gets letters from Muslims around the world, including Muslims Middle Eastern countries that, officially, are hostile to Israel. Here is a sample (all spelling and grammatical errors retained from the originals):[46]

Bosnia: "Zionism is Jewish ethnic consciousness. Nobody can deprive any ethnicity to have its national dream. Zionism does not upset because there is no goal to exterminate anybody. Peace can come if we recognize Israel and Jews as legitimate inhabitants of the territory."

Sweden: "Hello the I am a 24 year old muslim guy living in Sweden whos is completly in love with the Jewish people and Israel. ... What bother my all the time when you hear

[45] Arabs for Israel Web site, http://www.arabsforisrael.com.
[46] All comments, and many more, viewable online at http://www.arabsforisrael.com/arabemails /2005archive.html.

arab and muslim leaders blaming all their misery on the jews insted off facing reality off their own mistakes. . . . May god truly Bless The Children if Israel. The most unfortunet and missunderstood people of the world."

Algeria: "I like israel and all the industrial countries and israel is the miracle of the history because the first one became a country is in 1948 and the others has a long time in the history but are nothing in world."

Egypt: "I know about Arabs For Israel and I do like that site a lot. Ever since i was a little child, i had a problem with how people view Israel. I always had Israeli friends when i went to Sinai, and i believe Israel is a country that we should be proud to have in our region and as our neighbor. I always noticed the way Palestinians always refused any peaceful move on Israel's part because the Koran tells them that the Jews are misleaders. They want to commit terrorism and then allow Israel to make peaceful moves and then they'll think it's because of their so-called 'resistance'."

Tunisa: "I have a full respect of the great Jewish people and friendly feelings toward Israel, the only democracy in the middle east."

Syria: "If we could put toghether the financial power of the arabs and the inteligence of the israeli people, we could move the world."

England: "I just wanted to say that I too believe that Israel has not only the right to exist but can be a positive partner in helping to bring democracy and reform to our people."

The point here is not to tout Israel, but say two things:

- Moderate Muslims who support Israel certainly would support a Christian state, too; and
- If there were a Christian state, moderate Muslims wishing to preach for peace, and against the jihadists, might not have to emigrate to America or Europe to do it; perhaps they would be able to seek sanctuary in the Christian state and speak from there.

Imagine regular television and radio broadcasts, from the safety of a Christian state, of testimony from, interviews with, and discussions among moderate Muslim Palestinians to counter the jihadist propaganda that inundates the Middle Eastern airwaves today. An ounce of that, I think, would do more to advance Middle Eastern peace than a ton of European "diplomacy."[47]

And, to repeat what I said moments ago, the Christian state, by its very existence as an example of the advantages of peace with Israel would strengthen the moderates' argument, perhaps even to the point where such people could speak freely — perhaps even run for office — in Judea, Samaria and Gaza.

"Sheikh of All Sheiks"

Here are some additional examples of how Muslims are cooperating with Israel *today* and thus, I believe, would be equally receptive to a Christian state. I see no reason to doubt that Muslims who not only did not oppose, but actively *helped* Israel in her War of Independence in 1948, would help Christian-staters, too. For example, earlier, I mentioned the Druze[48]--Muslims who helped Jewish Palestinians under the British Mandate and, with Israel's successful rebirth, became, and remain, loyal Israelis. One such, a Bedouin sheikh, Ouda Abu Muamar, 96, called the "sheikh of all sheiks," was honored recently by the Israeli government for 60 years of service to the state:

> Even before the establishment of Israel, Abu Muamar was reportedly in close contact with the Palmah [the Jewish Palestinian underground army during the British Mandate], aiding them in their anti-British insurgency.

*   *   *

---

[47] The quotes around "diplomacy" are sarcastic. What passes for "diplomacy" in most of the international community amounts to nothing more — or less — than pressuring Israel for new concessions, in addition to those she has already made, while requiring nothing of the Muslim Palestinians.
[48] See page 126.

Abu Muamar ... is one of the few Beduin—if not the only one—to hold a campaign ribbon for service in the Palmah and the War of Independence, as well as two separate awards from the president for service to the defense community and to the Beduin minority.

*   *   *

He also served as one of then-division commander Ariel Sharon's staff officers in the Yom Kippur War.

*   *   *

Abu Muamar was instrumental in encouraging young Beduin men to serve in the IDF, and set an example by making sure all of his sons enlisted.

*   *   *

"We are all children of Abraham our Father," Abu Muamaar said ... "And we must live in peace."

I see no reason why such modern enlightened Muslims as the Arabs for Israel, Ouda Abu Muamara and Abu Muamara's children, so supportive of Israel, would not support a Christian state, too.

"Reforming Islam" and the Christian State

Ever since 9/11 put the threat of Islamic extremism on the world's front page, many people, within and without Islam have called on Muslims to "reform" their religion. No such reformation appears to be forthcoming, and experience, both historical and contemporary,[49] has shown that potential

---

[49] For example, the pardoning of the Afghani Christian convert (sentenced to death) and of the British teacher (sentenced to whipping) arrested in Sudan for letting a student name a teddy bear Mohammed were the result of Western pressure, not from Islam. At various times throughout history, enlightened Muslims have tried to reform their religion; sadly, every attempt has failed. Earlier, I mentioned the failure of reform to take hold in 19th century Egypt. (See page 44.) For example, writes Efraim Karsh, "All attempts to reorganize and modernize the [Ottoman] empire by equalizing the status of its non-

reformers have their work cut out for them. Fortunately, numerous examples, such as the ones I cite in this book, show that Muslims are perfectly able to coexist peacefully with Jews and Christian, without changing even one word of the Koran.

Dubai as an Example of Muslim Moderation

Above, I was talking about Muslim coexistence with Jews and applying the logic of that coexistence to Christians. But we need not speculate because there exists, in the tiny emirate of Dubai, a perfect example of the potential for comity between Islam and Christendom. As Max Boot and Lee Wolosky, who recently visited Dubai, note:

> While there is undoubtedly jihadist sentiment in the [United Arab Emirates], . . . what is notable is how far this small state has managed to move beyond many of the pathologies that mar its neighbors. [50]

While nearby Saudi Arabia forbids, and severely punishes, the mere possession of a Bible or the display of any Christian symbol, Dubai does precisely the opposite, actually *helping* Christians to celebrate their holy days. Here is one journalist's description of Christmas—yes, Christmas—in Dubai:

> With Santa Clauses in trendy malls, giant evergreen trees in hotels and holiday treats on supermarket shelves, Christmas cheer can't be missed . . . . Holiday kitsch is at an all-time high

<hr>

Muslim subjects backfired as the Muslim populations were loath to compromise on their superior position in any way. A royal decree in 1839 . . . triggered a violent revolt . . . which the authorities were unable to suppress for eleven years." Another, issued in 1856, "sparked widespread riots . . . which reached their horrific apogee in the spring and summer of 1860 [when] [b]etween twenty and twenty-five thousand Christians were brutally slaughtered . . ., while thousands perished of starvation and diseases and another hundred thousand were forcefully dislocated. Women were seized for harems; mothers were forced to sell their children." Efraim Karsh, *Islamic Imperialism*, 92-93.
[50] Max Boot and Lee Wolosky, "What to Do in Riyadh: You're only two hours from the Emirates—get on a plane," *The Weekly Standard*, December 10, 2007.

in Dubai, where many residents revel in the commercial hype of the Christian holiday.[51]

Another writer describes one hotel's Christmas festivities:

At the Le Meridien near the Airport every evening from 7 pm you can listen to Christmas Carols performed by The Le Meridien Dubai chorus. You can get [in]to the spirit of Christmas with the festive favorites in the menu: eggnog, glue wine, hot chestnuts and mince pies. Santa is visiting for [a] few minutes too and giving the kids presents.[52]

It is Dubai's example that informs my belief that all the back-and-forth about Islam—whether it is or is not a "religion of peace"—with each side quoting this or that passage from the Koran, the haditha of Mohammed, historical examples and so on, is a waste of time. In the first place, if nothing less than a total reform of Islam will defeat the jihadists, then we in the enlightened countries are in for a long, brutal struggle and we'd best dispense with diplomatic niceties and get about it ASAP. But second, and more important, as I just said, Dubai's example shows that interfaith comity between Islam and non-Islam is possible today, regardless of what is in the Koran, so what is in the Koran is irrelevant. Whether one feels *bound* to the Koran is, of course, another matter, and that, I submit, is the real problem.

But I'll leave that discussion to someone else. What matters here is that Muslim-Christian comity is not only possible, but an established fact and that, in my opinion, makes Muslim support of a Christian state not only possible, but, in some Muslim quarters, quite probable.

The Benefits of Accommodation

The obvious advantages Dubai enjoys from her friendly relations with other faiths provides strong evidence of equal, if

[51] "Merry Christmas Dubai," *Forbes*. I could not find the original article, but the quote is cited and can be found at http://christmasdubai.blogspot.com. (emphasis added)
[52] Ibid.

not greater advantages to be derived *by Muslims*, from a Christian state.

What advantages accrue from Dhabi's willingness to engage on friendly terms with non-Muslims, despite the Koran's and orthodox Islam's strictures against? Terry Carter and Lara Dunston, two travel-guide writers who actually live in Dubai, describe the emirate as

> a 21st-century phenomenon. From a small trading centre just 40 years ago to the international travel hub, tourist destination and business powerhouse it is today, its fortunes head skywards with still no end in sight.[53]

Max Boot and Lee Wolosky agree:

> Emirati men still dress in flowing robes and many women still cover their hair if not their faces. But it is also common to see European women ... parading around in high-cut skirts and low-cut blouses. And even many of the black-clad women wear jeans and high heels that peek out from under their black gowns. In some other predominantly Muslim cities such behavior could provoke a lashing; in Dubai no one bats an eyelash. Liquor is readily available in bars and restaurants ... The party doesn't even have to stop during Ramadan.[54]

And the result?

> A drive into town along a traffic-clogged highway takes a visitor past glass-and-steel skyscrapers too numerous to count Some are complete, others still under construction. Giant

---

[53] Terry Carter and Lara Dunston.
[54] Max Boot and Lee Wolosky.

cranes are everywhere: Dubai is estimated to have up to 25 percent of the world total.[55]

Meanwhile, if Judea, Samaria and Gaza have 25% of anything, it is 25% of the world's misery—a misery brought down on themselves, by themselves, in their refusal to emulate Dubai. Were they to exchange their medieval religious bigotry for Dubai's modern, enlightened approach, Judea, Samaria and Gaza could be reaping the same benefits, in terms of tourism and benefits, as Dubai—and, for that matter, Israel. (And remember, Dubai, to my knowledge, has no famous Christian or Jewish religious shrines or historical sites; Judea and Samaria, on the other hand, are full of them.)

Muslims Already Endorse a Three-State Solution

During discussions in Jerusalem and Ramallah in June 2007, shortly after Hamas's takeover of Gaza, Muslim participants from Judea and Samaria surprised Dennis Ross, the former special Middle East coordinator under President Bill Clinton, with an "interesting proposal":

> Let's make the West Bank work—socially, economically and institutionally—then hold up our model of success in contrast to the failure of Gaza ... Let Hamas preside over a dysfunctional, lawless state. We will build our own. Let's create understandings with Jordan *and Israel* for at least economic confederation and security. And if Hamas still hangs on in Gaza, *perhaps there can be a "three-state solution."*[56]

Apparently, my proposed partition plan, like my earlier proposal for establishing a Christian state in southern Lebanon, is not as radical as it might at first seem. Here we have Muslim Palestinians advocating the separation of Judea and Samaria from

---

[55] Ibid.
[56] Dennis Ross, "The Specter of 'Hamastan,'" *Washington Post*, June 4, 2007. (emphasis added)

Gaza. How then, can these same Muslim Palestinians logically oppose the separation of Judea from Samaria? And how, except out of religious bigotry, can these Muslim Palestinians object to Judea becoming a Christian state? After all, two of the three areas, Samaria and Gaza, would be Muslim—and remember, there are already, today, 22 Muslim Middle Eastern states, but *not one* Christian state despite the presence of 14 *million* Christians in the Middle East. Contrast that state of affairs with 4.5 million Jews, who *do* have a state.

The point is, given the size of the Middle East, the number of Muslims (over 200 million) and the number of existing Muslim Middle Eastern states (22), only jihadist Muslims, confronting another obstacle in implementing Mohammed's deathbed command , "Let there not be two religions in Arabia."[57]

Everyone else—Christians, Jews and, yes, all Muslims *except* the jihadists—would benefit enormously.

---

[57] Bernard Lewis, *The Crisis of Islam: Holy War and Holy Terror* (New York: Random House Trade Paperbacks, 2004), xxix.

Let us have faith that right makes might; and in
that faith let us to the end dare to do our duty as we
understand it — Abraham Lincoln

We make history and changing it is within our
power. — Ronald Reagan

I have made the strongest argument I can for the justness
of a Middle Eastern Christian state. Now I must convince
those of you who have stuck with me this far that it is
possible, as a practical matter, to establish such a state. I will
do this in the classic manner: by citing successful precedent,
and by proposing practical, clearly physically executable
(provided the political will is there) steps.

Israel as Prior Example

The best way to prove that a new thing *can* be done is to
show that a similar thing, in the same place, under similar
conditions, *has* been done. For purposes of establishing a
Christian state, the obvious example, of course, is the Jewish
state, Israel. Clearly, there are enough similarities between
the Jewish Palestinians' situation in 1947, the year before the
Jews re-declared their independence and reclaimed
sovereignty over their own land after 2,000 years of pagan,
Christian and Muslim occupation; and the Christian
Palestinians' situation today. Which is not to say that there
are not differences, too, but I think Christian state supporters
will be pleasantly surprised to learn that these differences
work very much to the Christian Palestinians' advantage.

One, perhaps the greatest, advantage is, of course, Israel herself. Obviously, in 1947, the Jewish Palestinians did not have a vibrant and successful Israel to look at as both proof that their dream could be achieved, and to serve as a practical example of how to achieve it. The Christian state founders, of course, will. They, unlike the Zionists, will not have to learn by trial and error; they will be able to study Israel's re-genesis, learn from both her successes and her missteps, and ideally (and ideally in consultation with Israel) add some new twists of their own.

Equally, if not more important than having Israel as an example, the Christian state founders would have her as a *neighbor*. At the very least, it means one direction fewer from which to be attacked by Muslims bent on strangling the nascent state in her crib, as they tried to do to Israel. More likely, Israel's military strength, especially if formalized by Israel's immediate recognition of the Christian state and written military alliance (in the same ceremony, if possible), would discourage *any* attack, from *any* direction. Even better, imagine Israel equipping, training and conducting exercises with a Christian army *before* the state is born. The army would be built and bivouacked in Israel, ready to move in, supplemented by Israeli troops if necessary, the instant the Christian state declares herself.

Population

In 1947, there were slightly over 11 million Jews[1] in the entire world—only 11 million Jews to advocate, fund and above all, populate a Jewish state. And yet, even with such a small pool from which to draw, enough Jews returned to their ancient homeland to reverse 2,000 years of pagan,

---

[1] Figure estimated from population date for 1945 and 1950, from various editions of the *American Jewish Yearbook*. Available online at http://www.jafi.org.il/education/100/concepts/demography/demtables.html. Scroll down to Table 2.

Muslim and Christian occupation to become the majority once more.

Now if the Jews could accomplish that from a pool of only 11 million, what could Christians do with a pool of 2.6 *billion*? Just do the math: 4.5 million Jewish Israelis, out of today's total worldwide population of 14 million, is a tad over 31 percent; a *single* percent of 2.6 billion Christians is *26 million*. *Half* of that one percent is 13 million and even a mere *tenth* of that one percent is still 2.6 *million* – more than enough to populate a Christian state. And, again going by Israel's example, a Christian Palestinian (or whatever they choose to rename themselves, as the Jewish Palestinians did), that initial population, whatever it is, can be expected to at least triple over the next 60 years; indeed, I would not be surprised to see it *more* than triple.

We can apply the same reasoning to tourism. Even today, if not for the Muslim Palestinians' holy war against the Jews, tourism to Judea, Samaria and Gaza would be much greater. I can attest to this personally, having toured Judea, Samaria and Gaza in 1968, only a year after Israel's victory in the Six Day War. After only one year of Israeli administration – and two decades before the infestation by Arafat and his jihadist cockroaches – the locals were already benefiting from a vibrant tourist industry undoubtedly fueled not only by the security the area enjoyed, but by the ease with which tourists, both Christian and Jewish, could move among Israel, Judea and Samaria, and Gaza. Without Arafat, the PLO, Fatah, Hamas, Islamic Jihad, the Al Aqsa Martyrs Brigade, et al., no security wall was needed to separate Israel from her former provinces and from Gaza so, of course, the security wall did not exist.

Funding

The enormous Christian numbers that would make populating the newborn Christian state so much easier than was populating the reborn Jewish one, would also guarantee Christians a much easier time financing their state than the Jews had in funding theirs. Just placing "Christian state fund" collection cans in churches, stores restaurants could raise tens, perhaps even hundreds of millions of dollars. And don't forget the Christian tradition of tithing: Imagine just a fraction of the world's Christians, especially wealthy Christians, tithing even a small percentage of their annual earnings to a fund set up exclusively to establish and support a Christian state.

To get just an inkling of Christian fundraising potential, consider that in just the first *two weeks* following the tsunami that ravaged the coastlines of South and Southeast Asia in 2004, worldwide *private* donations exceeded $2 *billion*.[2] Certainly, most of that money came from Christians.

But not all of it—which, to me, would imply the virtual certainty of additional funding from non-Christian sources Surely, in America at least, many non-Christians, such as myself, would welcome the chance to help our Christian friends build a Middle Eastern Christian state. And this very much includes Muslims, such as citizens and quite possibly even the governments of enlightened countries, such as Dubai.[3]

Finally, getting back to Christians, consider the so-called Christian Zionists. One Christian Zionist organization, Christians United for Israel, raised *$8.5 million* for Israel in a *single night*.[4] If that is how much Christian Zionists contribute to the Jewish state, how much would they contribute to the building of a *Christian state*—one that

---

[2] Emily Smith, "Private sector digs deep," *CNN*, January 12, 2005. Available online at http://www.cnn.com/2005/WORLD/asiapcf/01/12/tsunami.privateaid/indes.html.
[3] See page 164. Other enlightened countries, not mentioned in this book, are Abu Dhabi, Qatar, which recently allowed the construction of churches; and Bahrain, whose recently appointed ambassador to the U.S. is a Jewess.
[4] Saul Elbine, "Evangelicals rais $8.5 m. for Jewish state," *Jerusalem Post*, October 17, 2007.

would live in peace beside Israel and thus both spread the message, and provide an example, of peace?

And don't think I am talking only about charity. Imagine wealthy businessmen and entrepreneurs, who are *already* investing in Israel, being able to invest in a *Christian* state. For example, in 2006, Warren Buffett paid $4 billion for 80% of an Israeli company, Iscar Metalworking. Visiting Israel later that same year, he expressed his willingness to consider additional investments, saying, "Berkshire Hathaway and Israel will be here forever, as Israel and the US will be here forever."[5] As will Microsoft. And Intel. And IBM, Hewlett-Packard, Nokia, Motorola, and all the other companies worldwide that outsource to, and invest in, Israel. Not for nothing is Israel known as "Silicon Valley East,"[6]

In announcing Berkshire Hathaway's acquisition of Iscar, Warren Buffett said, "Being in Israel has a major advantage of having the exposure to a fabulous pool of talent and brains. When we bought Iscar, we bet on brains." Would it not be wonderful if Buffett could, someday, say the same about a *Christian* company, in a *Christian* state? Free the Christian Palestinians from the consequences of the jihadist Palestinians' holy war against the Jews, give them a secure area, with set borders within to flourish and prosper, and can anyone doubt that all the businesses betting on Jewish brains would be just as eager to bet on Christian ones? (And at the risk of stating the obvious, may I add that many of these investors would be Israelis?

There can be no doubt Christian state, living peacefully beside Israel, free from jihadist harassment, with an education system teaching love instead of hate, would

---

[5] Sharon Wrobel, "Buffett: Berkshire in Israel forever," *Jerusalem Post*, September 18, 2006.
[6] C.J. Prince, "Land of tech and honey: Israel is a quite leader in many tech fields, and is exporting much of its innovation," *The Chief Executive*, October 2004. Available online at http://findarticles.com/p/articles/mi_m4070/is_202/ai_n8576051/print.

quickly become an oases of investment—and enlightenment—just like Israel.

And might we also hope that *Muslim* Palestinians, seeing the prospering Christians next door, would decide that they wanted *their* piece of the pie, stop their "resistance" and adopt the Christian state's enlightened policies of peace and cooperation with Israel so that the Warren Buffets of the world could safely invest in Muslim brains, too?

Sympathetic Governments

It does not diminish the Jewish Palestinians' (now Israelis), who deserve tremendous credit for the work they have done and the results they have achieved in reclaiming their ancient kingdom from millennia of neglect by its pagan, Christian and Muslim occupiers, and transforming it into a modern democracy, to recognize that they could not have achieved so much, so fast, without the support of sympathetic foreign governments. Obviously significant was the United Nations vote that formally returned at least a portion of the Jewish homeland to its original and rightful owners. But just as, if not more, valuable, was the United States' immediate recognition of the reborn Israel, legitimizing her in the eyes of all but the most hostile and recalcitrant (so hostile and recalcitrant that they refuse to recognize Israel to this day) states virtually overnight.

Obviously, Israel being the only Jewish state, none of the leaders, or the majority populations, of the states that voted for and recognized Israel, was Jewish. Thus, the situation at the time of Israel's rebirth (and indeed, today) was that of a Jewish state seeking recognition from non-Jewish states.

The Christian-state founders, on the other hand, would have it much better, for theirs would be the happier circumstances of a *Christian* state seeking recognition *from other Christians*. And remember: these states have *already*, and for a long time, recognized Israel. Could any government that recognizes the Jewish state refuse to recognize the Christian one? More to the point, how could the *United States*, whose government not only recognized Israel, but was the first to do so, not recognize the Christian state? And when she does, the Christian state, like Israel before her, would gain instant legitimacy worldwide.

Nor would the Christian state founders need breathlessly to follow the tally of a UN vote, as Israel's restorers had to. Thanks, ironically, to the precedent set by the Muslim-majority state of Kosovo,[7] the Christian state will be able to declare independence unilaterally, bypassing the UN entirely.

Peace Treaties

Two of the most significant changes to occur in the Middle East since 1948 are the peace treaties Israel signed with Jordan and with Egypt. Would these two countries, formally at peace with Israel for more than a generation, attack a newly-declared Christian state, knowing that Israel almost certainly would enter the fight on the side of the Christians? Lebanon, of course, has no peace treaty with Israel, but the idea that Hezbollah would invade Israel to attack a Christian state declared in Judea is only slightly less absurd than the idea that the invasion would succeed. The idea that Syria, which dares not invade Israel to recover the Golan Heights, would invade Israel to prevent the establishment of a Christian state is also too ridiculous to consider seriously.

The bottom line is, unlike Israel, which at the instant of her rebirth, was attacked on all sides by hostile powers, the great likelihood is that the new Christian state—one that, if my advice is followed, would have an army of her own *and* a military alliance with Israel—*would not be attacked at all.*

[7] See page **Error! Bookmark not defined.**.

Needless to say, the ability to establish an independent state without the slightest fear of attack, would be a *major* improvement over the situation the Israelis faced.

The *practical* implication of this freedom from outside threats is enormous. It means that, as I am writing these words, today, this very minute, there is no *practical* obstacle to creating a Middle Eastern Christian State *today*.

All that is needed is the political will to do it.

Come Back, Israel!

A final, and important "advantage" present day Christian Palestinians have over their Jewish Palestinian predecessors is the Christian Palestinians' greater—much greater—suffering under the Palestinian Authority than what the Jewish Palestinians endured under the British Mandate. The greater the suffering, obviously, the more compelling the argument for taking bold steps to end it.

The strongest argument for freeing Christian Palestinians from their subjugated status under Muslim Palestinian rule comes, ironically, from the Muslim Palestinians themselves. And here I do not mean, as you might think, the Muslims running the Palestinian Authority or Hamas; I am talking about the Muslim Palestinians who, like the Christian Palestinians, are forced to live under, and suffer the consequences of, Muslim Palestinian (mis)governance.

How bad is life for Muslim Palestinians under their fellow Muslim Palestinians? Bad enough that increasing numbers of them frankly acknowledge that they were better off under the Israelis and have *openly called for Israel to come back*. According to recent article in *The New York Times*,

> [A] few Palestinian columnists have broken a
> political taboo by referring to the Israeli occupation

as perhaps preferable to the chaos" that currently reigns in Judea, Samaria and Gaza.[8]

Faiz Abbas and Muhammad Awwad, journalists for *Al-Sinara*, an Arab Israeli weekly, write:

> People in Gaza are hoping that Israel will reenter the Gaza Strip, wipe out both Hamas and Fatah ... They also say that ... *they [have begun to] miss the Israelis*, since Israel is *more merciful* than [the Palestinian gunmen. [They said,] "Once, we resisted Israel together, but *now we call for the return of the Israeli army to Gaza.*"[9]

Yahya Rabah, whose column appears in the Palestinian paper, *Al-Hayat Al-Jadida*, writes:

> If a government that includes Fatah, Hamas, other factions and independents ... has not been able to save the day, it means that no one can, *unless Israel decides that its army should intervene.* Then it will invade [the Gaza Strip], kill and arrest [people] — *but this time, not as an occupying [force] but as an international peace-keeping force.* Look what we have come to, how far we have deteriorated, and what we have done to ourselves."[10]

Another Palestinian journalist, Majed Azzam, writes:

> We should have the courage to acknowledge the truth. ... The [only] thing that prevents the chaos and turmoil in Gaza from spreading to the West Bank is the presence of the Israeli

[8] Isabel Kershner, "Anniversary of 1967 War Shows Lasting Divisions," *New York Times*, June 6, 2007.
[9] *Al-Sinara* (Nazareth), May 18, 2007. Translated by Middle East Media Research Institute and available on their Web site at http://memri.org/bin/opener.cgi?Page =archives&ID=IA35907. (emphases added)
[10] *Al-Hayat Al-Jadida* (Palestinian Authority), May 15, 2007. Translated by Middle East Media Research Institute and available on their Web site at http://memri.org/bin/opener.cgi?Page=archives&ID=IA35907. (emphasis added)

occupation" [in the West Bank] ... [as opposed
to] its absence from the Gaza Strip."[11]

And finally, Palestinian poet Bassem al-Nabris:

> If there was a referendum in the Gaza Strip [on
> the question of] "would you like the Israeli
> occupation to return?' half the population
> would vote "yes." ... But in practice, I believe
> the number of those in favor is *at least 70 percent,
> if not more.*[12]

In November 2007, ahead of yet another peace conference,
this time in Annapolis, when Israeli Prime Minister Ehud
Olmert expressed a willingness to cede certain Arab
neighborhoods in Jerusalem to the Palestinian Authority,
Muslim Israelis, suddenly faced with just the mere
suggestion that they might someday find themselves
governed by the PA, went into panic mode:

> Those feeling skittish about the city's potential
> partition aren't just Israelis ... *but also
> Palestinian Jerusalemites*, who fear that their
> standard of living will fall if they come under
> the control of the Palestinian Authority (PA).
>
> "I don't want to have any part in the PA. I
> want the health insurance, the schools, all the
> things we get by living here," says Ranya
> Mohammed as she does her afternoon shopping
> in Shuafat.
>
> "I'll go and live in Israel before I'll stay here
> and live under the PA, even if it means taking
> an Israeli passport," says Mrs. Mohammed,

[11] *Al-Risala* (Gaza), May 14, 2007. Translated by Middle East Media Research Institute and available on
their Web site at http://memri.org/bin/opener.cgi?Page =archives&ID=IA35907.
[12]   *Elaph* (Arabic electronic newspaper). Article available at http://www.elaph.com
/elaphweb/elaphwriter/2007/5/236709.htm. Translated by Middle East Media Research Institute and
available on their Web site at http://memri.org/bin/opener.cgi?Page =archives&ID=IA35907.
(emphasis added)

whose husband earns a good living doing business here. "I have seen their suffering in the PA. We have a lot of privileges I'm not ready to give up."

Nabil Gheet, a neighborhood leader who runs a gift and kitchenware outfit in the adjacent town of Ras Khamis, also resists coming under the PA's control.

"We have no faith in the Palestinian Authority. It has no credibility," he says, as his afternoon customers trickle in and out. "I do not want to be ruled by [Palestinian Authority President Mahmoud] Abbas's gang."[13]

My point here, simply, is this: If *Muslim* Palestinians do not want to live under Muslim Palestinian rule, why should we force *Christian* Palestinians to, if there is a way to free them? And I'll go even further: If it is possible to create a Christian state that could provide sanctuary to at least *some* Muslim Palestinians desperate to get out from under Muslim Palestinian control, how can we not provide it?

Jewish Palestinians, living under British, not Muslim, rule, could not make this argument. Christian Palestinians *can*.

The Bottom Line

Clearly, those who would establish a Christian state today would enjoy some significant advantages over the situation Israel's re-founders faced in 1947. I just listed some of the obvious ones; I'm sure some of you can think of others. Now here are a few practical suggestions — and again, I am confident that other, wiser minds came come up with additional, ideally even better, ones — on how to exploit these advantages to create a Middle Eastern state.

---

13 Ilene R. Prusher, "Israel puts Jerusalem on the negotiating table," *Christian Science Monitor*, November 6, 2007.

STEP ONE
RECOGNIZE THE CHRISTIANS

In a sincere world, with an international community that was consistent in its professed compassion for oppressed peoples, this first step should not be necessary. Unfortunately, due to the *insincere, inconsistent* world we *do* live in, it is.

Sadly, many, if not most, of you reading in the first part of this book about the plight of the persecuted Christians of Judea, Samaria and Gaza, and beyond, are reading about it for the first time. So absorbed is the international community in giving jihadist Muslims an Iranian proxy terrorist state on Israel's border from which to conduct, and escalate, their holy war against the Jews, that they willfully refuse even to acknowledge, let alone help, the Christians.

Christian Palestinians are truly a "stealth minority" — the people nobody sees, because they don't want to, for two reasons:

- Large portions of the citizenry of certain members of the international community — okay, England and France — are, at best, closet anti-Semites, openly sympathize with the Muslim Palestinians, wish Israel would disappear and delight in painting the Israelis/Zionists/Jews as the "bad guys" (even though many Muslim and Christian Israelis serve in the Israeli army). Which, conversely, must mean that the Muslim Palestinians are the "good guys." Shining a light on the persecution of Christian Palestinians and making the obvious comparison with Christian Israelis (for example, the Christian Palestinian population is declining; the Christian Israeli population is flourishing) would show quickly and undeniably, that it is the Muslim Palestinians are the "bad guys" and very bad, bad guys at that.

- If the persecution of Christian Palestinians under Muslim Palestinian rule — the boycotts; the church burnings; the land thefts; the rapes, the forced marriages, the kidnapping, the extortion, the murders, the use of Christian neighborhoods as staging grounds for jihadist attacks on Israel and as sanctuaries for jihadists fleeing Israeli justice — is allowed to become clear and undeniable, the idea of perpetuating their persecution, by putting them permanently under Muslim Palestinian subjugation, becomes abhorrent. Goodbye, two-state solution!

Thus, an international community — including, unfortunately, the U.S. State Department and even many Israelis, both Jewish and Christian — suffering from Oslo Syndrome[14], determined to impose their precious two-state solution, no matter whom it hurts, is not about to publicize the persecution of Christian Palestinians and the suffering they endure — and certainly would continue to endure in a Muslim-majority "Palestinian state," until Elias Freij's prophesy of Bethlehem becoming a town with churches but no Christians, is fulfilled.

Since the international community won't tell the truth, decent people such as you and I must do it for them and so, he first step in the campaign to establish a Middle Eastern Christian state, must be to call attention to both the existence and the suffering of Christian Palestinians in Judea, Samaria and Gaza and, of course, to make it crystal clear that it is Muslim Palestinians and not Israel, who is responsible for that suffering.

At the same time we are getting the world, and especially Christians, to see Christian Palestinians, we must get the world to see them *as a separate people*, distinct from Muslim Palestinians, to distinguish Christian Palestinians from

---

[14] See page 113.

Muslim Palestinians as readily as they already distinguish Muslim Palestinians from Jewish Palestinians (Israelis).

But we're not done yet, for once we've gotten good people to *see* the Christian Palestinians, we are faced with the more difficult task of getting people to *care* about them. How *much* should they care about them? Well, if the international community, heavily Christian, could care about their fellow Christians as much as they apparently care about *Muslims*, that would be a good start. Unfortunately, as Philip Jenkins points out:

> Western powers ... make no pretence of respecting confessional ties. During the Yugoslav crisis of the 1990s, the United States and Western Europe sided consistently with Muslim interests *against* the Christian Serbs, to the point of intervening militarily in Kosovo. . . . *At the same time, the oppressed Christians of the Sudan were receiving no support either from NATO, nor from any Western or Christian entity.* Even mainstream Western churches were unwilling to be too forthright in denouncing persecution.[15]

Is it too much to ask the many countries, including the U.S., that supported and now recognize Muslim Kosovo to support a *Christian* state?

The words of Jack, a Christian Palestinian, illustrates how little support Christian Palestinians get from their coreligionists, compared to what Jews and Muslims get from theirs:

> Jews [worldwide] support the ultra-Orthodox, who don't work but just study and have five children to a family. The Muslims have large extended families who help each other out, *and*

---

[15] Philip Jenkinsz, *The Next Christendom*, 218. (emphasis added)

even they receive help from churches. We're a small
community *and don't receive anything.*[16]

Apparently, none of the hundreds of millions of dollars
the world sends the Muslim Palestinians is not making it to
the Christians. So what can we do to make our leaders
(a) acknowledge the existence of persecuted Christians of
Judea, Samaria and Gaza and (b) do something to save
them?

The European Union, whose "Arab policy . . . aims at creating
a Euro-Arab economic and geostrategic continent conceived as a
counterbalance to American influence,"[17] may be too big a part of
the problem to be much help with the solution. That policy
abroad, combined with "Eurabia's" headlong rush into
dhimmitude at home, makes Europe's leaders more likely to help
the Muslims hide the Christian Palestinians' plight than to expose
it. And unless we're talking about French farmers dumping
vegetables on the highway and train conductors going on strike,
the major European powers are not exactly famous for being
responsive to pressure from the peasantry — uh, citizenry. EU HQ
in Brussels is even worse.

America, fortunately, is different. When we petition our
leaders, our leaders listen. Therefore, for us, the solution, as
clichéd as it sounds, is simple: Write your Congressman.
And Senator. Tell them to speak, on the House and Senate
floors, about the persecuted Christians of Judea, Samaria
and Gaza. Demand that a nice chunk of our foreign aid to
the "Palestinian people" go *directly* to the Christians,
bypassing the Palestinian Authority (and its officers' Swiss
bank accounts) entirely. Demand that the PA allow the
Christian Palestinians to create an agency, composed
entirely of Christians, to receive and disburse the funds
without interference from the PA (and — hint, hint — serve as
the provisional government of a future Christian state).

16 David Smith, "Christians Anonymous," *Jerusalem Post*, January 31, 2008.
17 Ye'or, "Israel, Christianity, and Islam: The Challenge of the Future."

But most of all, we must demand of our representatives that they oppose, with speeches *and legislation*, the two-state solution and support, instead, a *multi-state solution* that includes a Christian state.

This year, 2008, being an election year, I can think of no better time to begin. And, while we're on the subject, don't neglect the presidential candidates. Should you be find yourself at a rally of "town hall meeting," with the opportunity to ask your candidate a question, ask for a Christian Middle Eastern state.

Do you remember Walid Phares's quote that appears near the beginning of this book?

> [A]s far as the 'peace process' is concerned,
> Christians are notable by their absence!

Let us work together to ensure that, in the next Camp David negotiation, the Christian Palestinians of Judea, Samaria and Gaza are notable by their *presence*.

STEP TWO
STOP THE TWO-STATE SOLUTION

I just mentioned—indeed, it's the reason I wrote this book—the need to replace the two-state solution with a multi-state solution that includes a Christian state. However, so wedded is the international community to the two-state solution, that it deserves separate treatment.

That the international community, especially our craven Eurabian friends, is obsessed with the two-state solution is as undeniable as the reason for their obsession: Oslo Syndrome.[18] Oslo Syndrome, you'll recall, is the irrational beliefs that (1) peace in the Middle East depends entirely on

---

[18] See page 113.

Israel appeasing the jihadist Muslim Palestinians bent on her destruction, while the jihadist Muslim Palestinians need do nothing (except, of course, to follow up every Israeli concession with a new demand; and (2) that if Israel gives the jihadist Muslim Palestinians bent on her destruction a convenient platform from which to attack her, behind the borders of a sovereign "Palestinian state," Israel's enemies will become her friends.

Yeah, right.

Oslo Syndrome, we learned, results from Israel's and the international community's natural desire to—but totally irrational belief that they can—control a situation that, in fact, they cannot control. Peace will come to the Middle East when, and only when the Muslim Palestinians, decide that they want it and demonstrate their desire by changing *their* behavior, not by demanding that Israel change hers. When Muslim Palestinian demands for land are replaced with requests for peace, there will be peace and not before.

The (Muslim) "Palestinian-state movement" is not an "oppressed people's" quest for self-determination, but a canard to mask what is, in fact, a holy war against the Jews. The British Mandate comprised land that is, today, Israel *and Jordan*. Ethnically, Jordan, today, is majority-Palestinian. (The ruling Hashemites are a minority.) Yet, we don't see Qassam rockets falling on *Jordan*, do we? We don't hear *any* call from Muslim Palestinians to "liberate" *Jordan*. Indeed, we don't even hear any calls—not even from George Bush, who has made the promotion (read, creation) of democracy in the Muslim Middle East the hallmark of his administration—simply to demand that King Abdullah allow democracy in Jordan. Were the Palestinian majority to demand, and get, the right to vote, they could vote the king out, a representative, *majority-Palestinian* government in, rename Jordan "Palestine" and have their "Palestinian state" virtually overnight. Instead, they choose to attack Israel.

Purely as a practical matter, the Muslim Palestinians no more need East Jerusalem in order to leave peacefully, and prosper, than Western Germany needed East Berlin to create their so-called economic miracle. In the two decades of Israeli "occupation" of her own former provinces and her occupation of the Gaza Strip, Palestinians had no problem commuting to and from jobs in Israel without the eastern portion of Israel's eternal capital becoming the capital of a "Palestinian state." There is no reason, except for the security wall necessitated entirely *by Muslim Palestinian violence*, that they cannot do so again.

> *If one's goal truly is the Muslim Palestinians' and Christian Palestinians' welfare and not aiding and abetting the Muslim Palestinians' holy war against the Jews, then the demand must be that the Muslim Palestinians end their useless, self-destructive "resistance,"* **not** *that Israel surrender land.*

The question is, *how* to get the Muslim Palestinians to change their self-destructive—and Christian Palestinian-destructive—behavior? Fortunately, recent history provides the answer, a method with a 63-year record of proven success. At what, in historical time, qualifies as "about the same time," just three years before the Muslim Palestinians were bewailing their defeat in the Jewish Palestinians' 1948 War of Independence, two great nations were suffering the effects of a much greater defeat, in World War II. Judea, Samaria and Gaza did not experience anything even approaching the destruction wreaked on Nazi Germany and imperial Japan. Yet look at those two countries today: Both are peaceful and prosperous, while Judea-Samaria-Gaza remains a basket case.

What accounts for this difference? What have the Germans and Japanese — and the Israelis! — been doing for the past 63 years that the Muslim Palestinians have not?

They have been rebuilding their countries, that's what. While the Muslim Palestinians have spent much of the time since 1948 wallowing in Jew-hatred and dreams of reversing their loss, the Germans and Japanese made peace with the victorious Allies long ago and put their energy and passion into creating probably the two greatest miracles of economic achievement the world has ever seen.

We could come up with any number of reasons why the Germans and Japanese on the one hand, and the Muslim Palestinians on the other, chose such divergent paths, but only one need concern us here: Germany and Japan abandoned their dreams of conquest when it was made absolutely clear to them that *the dreams could never be achieved*. The leaders who led the citizenry into a disastrous war and didn't die in the War were discredited, driven from power and, in some cases, tried and executed. But most of all, both powers were *decisively defeated* — so decisively that no German or Japanese in his right mind dreams of resurrecting the German Reich or the Japanese Empire.

Now compare that state of affairs to the Middle East, where Israel has found herself, more than once, on the verge of defeating her enemies *and has been pressured, every time, from dealing the decisive blow* that would end the Muslim Palestinian dreams of conquest. Germany and Japan are prosperous because the Allies decisively defeated her enemies and, equally if not more important, *dictated the peace*. In both countries, the Allies made sure that the new leaders would be pacifists and not warmongers, dictated their form of government — and in Japan, *we even changed their religion*. No longer was the Emperor a living deity for whom Japanese citizens were required to sacrifice their lives.

But today, the same powers who dealt so decisively with *their* enemies prevent Israel, most recently in the 2006 Lebanon war, from dealing decisively with *hers*.

The international community apparently thinks that, by restraining Israel, by refusing to allow her to *win*, they are promoting peace. But what they are really doing is allowing Fatah and Hamas—who, unlike, the Nazi Party, are allowed to rule—to continue to harbor the hope that they can, in time, achieve their dream of destroying Israel.

And the result? Year after year, for 63 years and counting, the people of Germany and Japan prosper, while the Muslim Palestinians stagnate. And of course, the Christian Palestinians, powerless under the Muslim-dominated Palestinian Authority and Hamas, have no choice but to stagnate right along with them. But what if Christian Palestinians were allowed to pursue their *own* course? Which would example would they emulate—Germany's and Japans', or the Muslim Palestinians'?

I think you know the answer; which brings us right back to Oslo Syndrome and the international community's perverse obsession with creating a "two-state solution." Let's be brutally honest: The only thing the two-state solution would do for (or should that be, "to"?) *Christian* Palestinians, is to make their current situation suffering under the Palestinian Authority permanent—or at least until Bethlehem becomes Elias Freij's "town with churches but no Christians."

The first order of business, then, for we who care about the welfare of the Christians of Judea, Samaria and Gaza—and, incidentally, of whether one advocates a Christian state, is to *stop the two-state solution.*

I, of course, belief that the best course is the creation of a Christian state, preferably from Judea. But that subject can be argued later, after the Christian Palestinians are safe, even if ensuring their safety means that Israel must, at least temporarily, retake Judea, Samaria and Gaza—as, we have seen, even many Muslim Palestinians want.[19]

STEP THREE
REROUTE THE SECURITY WALL

The best way to protect the Christian Palestinians is to do what Israel has done so successfully to protect herself: build a security wall, between Christian Palestinians and Muslim Palestinians, to separate, and thus protect, the former from the latter.

Of course, the new security wall that would prevent Muslim Palestinians from threatening Christian Palestinians, would also prevent these same Muslim Palestinians from threatening *Jewish* Palestinians (Israelis). But what about the places where the existing security wall, if nothing is done, would continue to keep out *Christian* Palestinians, who are nonviolent, do not participate in the Muslim Palestinians' holy war against the Jews and pose absolutely no threat to Israel? The answer is as just as it is obvious:

The answer is as just as it is obvious:

> *As the new wall separating Christian Palestinians from Muslim Palestinians goes up, the old wall, where it separates Christian Palestinians from Muslim Palestinians can—indeed,* must—*come down.*

The practical business of building the new security wall should be no more difficult than was building the current one. Indeed, it may be possible, simultaneously, to create the new wall and bring down the old one, simply by rerouting

---

[19] See pages 176 to 178.

all or part of the current wall—essentially, taking a portion of the wall where it runs south down from Jerusalem and "swinging" it north to extend eastward along the line between Judea and Samaria. Gaza, of course, is already separated from Judea by miles of Israeli territory.

The immediate benefits to Christian Palestinians of being (1) released from Muslim subjugation; (2) taken out of the crossfire between Muslim Palestinian jihadists and Israel and (3) having access, once again, to Israeli jobs, trade and capital, are obvious. But Muslim Palestinians can benefit as much, or even more, if seeing their Christian Palestinian neighbors, enjoying the security and prosperity that comes from comity and cooperation with the Israelis, inspires them to emulate the Christian Palestinians and make their own peace with Israel.

STEP FOUR
A CHRISTIAN RIGHT OF RETURN

As did Israel in 1948, the new Christian state will need to rebuild and then increase population to quickly erase, and ultimately reverse, their numerical disadvantage vis-à-vis Muslims. As has proved true for the Jewish Palestinians (Israelis), only a demographic playing field tilted heavily in the Christian Palestinians' favor can ensure their safety, their prosperity and, above all, their liberty. Only through superior numbers can Christian Palestinians live without fearing a return to dhimmitude.

Key to this demographic revival is a very liberal immigration policy *for Christians*. In a nutshell, the new Christian state must adopt its own counterpart to Israel's famous "law of return," whereby, except for the most extreme cases, any Christian setting foot on Christian state soil is granted immediate asylum and citizenship. Conversely, admittance and naturalization for non-Christians would be sufficiently restricted to guarantee an overwhelmingly Christian majority.

Also, obviously, even within the context of a very liberal Christian immigration policy, special preference must be given to converts, who routinely suffer even more than born Christians in many Muslim states and in India. Earlier, we met "Hannah,"[20] the British imam's daughter who was forced into hiding after receiving death threats after she converted to Christianity. Hannah is by no means unique. Death threats have also forced 22-year-old Dutch Muslim apostate Ehsan Jami, who left Islam after the 2001 World Trade Center attack, to go into hiding.

Hannah has already converted; Ehsan may or may not wish to convert. But both should be granted asylum in the Christian state—and, ideally, allowed to broadcast, from Christian state television and radio stations, to their fellow converts and potential converts, around the world.

STEP FIVE
THE CHRISTIAN AGENCY

Anyone can have a dream. Throughout 2,000 years of exile during which their land was conquered and re-conquered, occupied and reoccupied, by successive waves of Pagans, Christians and Muslims, Jews continued to dream of one day reclaiming of their stolen homeland, ending their prayer books and religious services with the bold declaration/promise, "Next year in Jerusalem." But it took a visionary, Theodor Herzl, to conceive a *practical plan* for turning an ancient dream into a modern reality. Indeed, as

---

[20] See page 102.

some of you may already have guessed, it is in homage to Herzl that I call this book *The Christian State*, after Herzl's earlier book, the one that led to Israel's rebirth, *The Jewish State (Der Jüdenstaat)*.

Just as I have emulated Herzl's title, we who would found a Christian state would do well to read Herzl's book and where possible emulate Herzl's methods.

Zionist History 101

As I've said, we Jews have dreamed of regaining our homeland virtually from the moment we were forced out; but we can trace the start of the modern Zionist movement to the courtyard of the École Militaire in Paris, where on the morning of January 5, 1895, a crowd gathered to watch the public degradation of Captain Alfred Dreyfus, convicted, falsely, in a secret trial, on the basis of fabricated evidence, of treason—the infamous Dreyfus Affair.

Among the witnesses to this disgraceful event was a young correspondent for the Vienna *Neue Freie Presse*, named Theodor Herzl. As Herzl watched Dreyfus's degradation within the courtyard's walls—and heard the crowds chanting "Death to the Jews!" outside, Herzl experienced an epiphany. Concluding, in that fateful moment, that Jews had no future in Europe (and, in my opinion, for what it's worth, still do not), Herzl, until that moment a thoroughly assimilated European Jew, was transformed into a passionate Zionist on the spot. Within six months, he had finished the first draft of *The Jewish State* and called on prominent Jews to convene a Zionist Congress "as a symbolic Parliament for those in sympathy with the implementation of Zionist goals."

The first Zionist Congress met on August 29, 1897, in Basel, Switzerland, where the participants boldly declared their purpose: "to create for the Jewish people a home in Eretz Israel[21] secured by law" through:

- The promotion by appropriate means of the settlement in Eretz-Israel of Jewish farmers, artisans, and manufacturers.
- The organization and uniting of the whole of Jewry by means of appropriate institutions, both local and international, in accordance with the laws of each country.
- The strengthening and fostering of Jewish national sentiment and national consciousness.
- Preparatory steps toward obtaining the consent of government, where necessary, in order to reach the goals of Zionism.[22]

Two years later, the Zionist Congress established its operating arm, the Jewish Agency, to implement the practical steps that would "encourage settlement of *Eretz Yisrael* (Hebrew for "Land of Israel") and enlist international Jewish support for development projects."[23]

Now take another look at the four bullet-points above, but this time, substitute the word, "Christian," for "Jewish," and "Christendom" for "Jewry." As Herzl, more than a century ago, saw no future for Jews in Europe, Christians need to ask themselves what kind of future they see for Christians in Judea, Samaria, Gaza, Lebanon, Egypt, Iraq and many other Muslim countries. Then they need to ask themselves whether it is time for world Christendom to take a page out of Herzl's book and convene a *Christian* "Zionist Congress." As you can probably guess, my personal answer is, "yes."

---

[21] "Eretz" means "land" in Hebrew — thus, "Land of Israel."
[22] "The First Zionist Congress and the Basel Program," *Jewish Virtual Library*, http://www.jewishvirtuallibrary.org/jsource/Zionism/First_Cong_&_Basel_Program.html. For those readers unfamiliar with Hebrew, "Eretz Israel" means "Land of Israel."
[23] *Zionist Glossary*, The Jewish Agency for Israel. Available online at http://www.jafi .org.il/education/100/gloss/index.html

At the very first meeting of the new Christian Zionist Congress, as one of its first items of business, the Congress, again taking its cue from Herzl and the original Zionist Congress, should create its own version of Herzl's Jewish Agency, a *Christian* Agency, to "encourage settlement of Judea (or whatever location is selected as the site of the nascent Christian state) and enlist international *Christian* support for development projects."

Basically, the Christian Agency, echoing its Jewish predecessor, would serve as the Christian Zionist Congress's executor arm. For example, it would be representatives of the Christian Agency, acting on behalf of the Christian Zionist Congress, who would solicit and manage funds; meet and coordinate with governments, non-governmental organizations and private citizens; handle public and press relations — in short, do all the things necessary to further the Christian Zionist Congress's goal of establishing a Christian state.

FINAL THOUGHTS

Reasonable people can disagree on *how* to create a Middle Eastern Christian state, but it is my fervent hope that, in this book, I have at least settled, in the affirmative, the question of *whether* to create one. But more important than proving that it *should* be done, indeed *must* be done, I hope I have convinced you that it *can* be done, if only a sufficient number of us have the will to do it.

There are, as far as I can see, no *practical* barriers standing in the way of a Christian Middle East state. Israel, with her military might, and the support of 2.6 *billion* Christians, could do it today. It therefore behooves Christians, and non-Christians too, if they care about the persecution of Christians, to urge Israel to act, to promise her our full support, and, through pressure on our leaders, guarantee that any United Nations resolutions intended to stop her from doing the right thing will be vetoed by the United States. At the same time, Israel, taking full advantage of the political cover we have given her, must be willing to seize the day and act boldly, to carve out and secure a Christian enclave, preferably in Judea, so that the Christian Palestinians, as I am sure they will desire, can dedicate their Savior's birthplace, Bethlehem, as the Christian state's capital. In so acting, Israel — and we who support her — must make it crystal clear, to the world, that the land Israel retakes, she retakes not for herself, but to *give away*, to Christians.

Christians around the world, for their part, must emulate America's Christians (and, I predict, incidentally, her Jews) and pressure their governments not to interfere with Israel's actions and, ideally, to support them, to add their voices to America's providing Israel an even stronger geopolitical umbrella under which to operate. Christians whose countries sit on the UN Security Council need to pressure their governments to join the U.S. in vetoing any and all anti-Israel resolutions intended to stop Israel from protecting the Christians of Judea, Samaria and Gaza the only way they *can* be protected: by enabling them to protect *themselves* in their own state. Indeed, Security Council members should be submitting resolutions *endorsing* Israel's efforts to save the persecuted Christians of Judea, Samaria and Gaza and of the world beyond.

Christians also need to start collecting and disbursing funds directly to the Christian Palestinians to help them *today* and to finance the building of the state. Forgive me for hurting my Christian friends, but your lack of support for Christian Palestinians—or for that matter, all persecuted Christians worldwide—in light of the aid you have lavished on Jews and Muslims, is shameful.

And finally, Christians who support a Christian state need to *go there*. Though the New Testament contains no Christian equivalent to the Koran's requirement that every Muslim, at least once in his lifetime, visit Mecca, nothing prevents each Christian from making and fulfilling a *personal* commitment to visit Bethlehem—to commune with his coreligionists in the Holy Land, pray with tem in their churches and, above all, show them that they are not alone.

But most of all, the world's Christians must work to give themselves what Jews and Muslims have, *their own state*, one that will:

- Insulate Christian Palestinians from the Muslims "resistance" in which Christian Palestinians play no part;
- Protect Christian Palestinians from Muslim violence;
- Ensure the security and integrity of Christian holy sites;
- Allow Christian women to dress as they please and to go where they will, day or night;
- Provide sanctuary for the world's persecuted Christians, by guaranteeing every Christian an Israeli-style "right of return," including automatic citizenship;
- Serve as a haven and spiritual homeland for Christians who wish to totally immerse themselves in a Christian lifestyle among Christendom's holiest sites, to worship where their Savior worshipped, to walk where He walked; and above all,
- *Allow Christians to make a separate peace with Israel independently of, and without interference from, Muslim Palestinians.*

In 1776, in his pamphlet, *Common Sense*, with these words, Thomas Paine urged his fellow Americans to take the audacious step of separating from England and transforming 13 colonies into 13 independent states:

> Every thing that is right and natural pleads for separation. The blood of the slain, the weeping voice of nature cries, *'tis time to part*.

Today, "everything that is right and natural pleads" for *another* separation, of Christian Palestinians from Muslim Palestinians. Today, "the blood of the slain, the weeping voice of nature cries," once again, that 'tis time to part—and to *partition.* The time has come for the Middle East's Christians to take their rightful placed alongside the other two great Middle Eastern faiths, as a *separate* people, with their *own* culture, their *own* aspirations — and above all, their own right to self-determination *in their own state.*

www.ingramcontent.com/pod-product-compliance
Lightning Source LLC
Chambersburg PA
CBHW022106280326
41933CB00007B/273